NIV / NAS

It All Begins With Genesis

TEACHER

Petersburg, Kentucky, USA

It All Begins With Genesis
Teacher Book NIV/NAS

A Student Book should be purchased for each student, whether in the Christian school classroom or in the homeschool environment. In a classroom setting, always order one extra for the teacher so that you have copies of everything for reference. Students will take home the pages of the Student Book throughout the study.

First printing: Janurary 2010

ISBN: 1-60092-296-1

Author: Sheila Richardson
Cover desgin and interior layout: Diane King

You may contact the author:
Sheila Richardson
3474 Dunrovin Farm
Crozet, VA 22932
434-823-4438
dunrovin@esinet.net

Printed in China

www.answersingenesis.org

Table of Contents

It All Begins With Genesis

Introduction

This course consists of 34 lessons. It is designed to fit the average year-long Sunday school curriculum. If a shorter course is desired, the origins/worldview section (lessons 12–19) may be used as a stand-alone study of origins and science within the biblical framework.

The subject matter is best suited to middle-school young people, grades 6–8. Children in grades 3–5 may also be capable of completing the lessons, but the concepts presented are better understood and applied by the older child. High-school students and even some adults could also benefit from the course. Some of the illustrations would need to be changed for the more mature student.

The course can be adapted successfully to a day-school curriculum that can be used in Christian schools or homeschool.

This course includes

- Student lessons that will be completed during each class. There is more material in each lesson than normally can be completed in a 45-minute class. This enables the teacher to pick and choose for enrichment as well as to assign home study, if desired.
- Teacher guides that include the goals for each lesson, the materials needed for the lesson, a suggested teaching plan and suggestions for activities and games that will accomplish the plan. The enclosed CD includes sample activities and masters that can be used with the lessons.

Three main goals

1. The first and major goal is that the student begins to build a solidly biblical worldview. Any worldview is most of all determined by a person's understanding of God. It is our desire to instill in the learner a love for God's Word and His world. It is also our goal to help the student discern the various worldviews that drive much of what he sees and hears in the secular culture.
2. The second goal is closely connected to the first. Since the book of Genesis (chapters

1–11) is the foundation for the Christian worldview, it will be the focus for our in-depth study. The origin of every doctrine of Christianity— Creation, Fall, judgment and redemption—is found in Genesis.

3. The final goal is that the student learns the principles of inductive Bible study. The message of Genesis will be revealed as inductive study is practiced. He will practice principles of Bible study that incorporate useful tools for observing, interpreting and applying the text. He will see for himself what the Word teaches. These tools, when developed, will serve him well throughout a lifetime of studying God's Word.

Integrating the Seven C's into Your Curriculum

Throughout *It All Begins with Genesis* you will see references to the Seven C's of History. You will find a 7 C's Connection in each lesson identifying how the lesson topic lines up with biblical history. Students will find this feature at the end of each lesson with blanks to fill in to demonstrate their understanding of the connections.

The Seven C's can be used to develop a biblical worldview in students, young or old. Much more than entertaining stories and religious teachings, the Bible has real connections to our everyday life. It may be hard, at first, to see how many connections there are, but with practice ,the daily relevance of God's Word will come alive. Let's look at the Seven C's of History and how each can be connected to what the students are learning.

Creation

God perfectly created the heavens, the earth, and all that is in them in six normal-length days around 6,000 years ago.

This teaching is foundational to a biblical worldview and can be put into the context of any subject. In science, the amazing design that we see in nature—whether in the veins of a leaf or the complexity of your hand—is all the handiwork of God. Virtually all of the lessons in *It All Begins with Genesis* can be related to God's creation of the heavens and earth.

Other contexts include:

Natural laws—any discussion of a law of nature naturally leads to God's creative power.

DNA and information—the information in every living thing was created by God's supreme intelligence.

Mathematics—the laws of mathematics reflect the order of the Creator.

Biological diversity—the distinct kinds of animals that we see were created during the Creation Week, not as products of evolution.

Art—the creativity of man is demonstrated through various art forms.

History—all time scales can be compared to the biblical time scale extending back about 6,000 years.

Ecology—God has called mankind to act as stewards over His creation.

Corruption

After God completed His perfect creation, Adam disobeyed God by eating the forbidden fruit. As a result, sin and death entered the world, and the world has been in decay since that time. This point is evident throughout the world that we live in. The struggle for survival in animals, the death of loved ones, and the violence all around us are all examples of the corrupting influence of sin.

Other contexts include:

Genetics—the mutations that lead to diseases, cancer, and variation within populations are the result of corruption.

Biological relationships—predators and parasites result from corruption.

History—wars and struggles between mankind, exemplified in the account of Cain and Abel, are a result of sin.

Catastrophe

God was grieved by the wickedness of mankind and judged this wickedness with a global Flood. The Flood covered the entire surface of the earth and killed all air-breathing creatures that were not aboard the Ark. The eight people and the animals aboard the Ark replenished the earth after God delivered them from the catastrophe.

The catastrophe described in the Bible would naturally leave behind much evidence. The studies of geology and of the biological diversity of animals on the planet are two of the most obvious applications of this event. Much of scientific understanding is based on how a scientist views the events of the Genesis Flood.

Other contexts include:

Biological diversity—all of the birds, mammals, and other air-breathing animals have populated the earth from the original kinds which left the Ark.

Geology—the layers of sedimentary rock seen in roadcuts, canyons, and other geologic features are testaments to the global Flood.

Geography—features like mountains, valleys, and plains were formed as the floodwaters receded.

Physics—rainbows are a perennial sign of God's faithfulness and His pledge to never flood the entire earth again.

Fossils—Most fossils are a result of the Flood rapidly burying plants and animals.

Plate tectonics—the rapid movement of the earth's plates likely accompanied the Flood.

Global warming/Ice Age—both of these items are likely a result of the activity of the Flood. The warming we are experiencing today has been present since the peak of the Ice Age (with variations over time).

Confusion

God commanded Noah and his descendants to spread across the earth. The refusal to obey this command and the building of the tower at Babel caused God to judge this sin. The common language of the people was confused and they spread across the globe as groups with a common language. All people are truly of "one blood" as descendants of Noah and, originally, Adam.

The confusion of the languages led people to scatter across the globe. As people settled in new areas, the traits they carried with them became concentrated in those populations. Traits like dark skin were beneficial in the tropics while other traits benefited populations in northern climates, and distinct people groups, not races, developed.

Other contexts include:

Genetics—the study of human DNA has shown that there is little difference in the genetic makeup of the so-called "races."

Languages—there are about seventy language groups from which all modern languages have developed.

Archaeology—the presence of common building structures, like pyramids, around the world confirms the biblical account.

Literature—recorded and oral records tell of similar events relating to the Flood and the dispersion at Babel.

Christ

God did not leave mankind without a way to be redeemed from its sinful state. The Law was given to Moses to show how far away man is from God's standard of perfection. Rather than the sacrifices, which only covered sins, people needed a Savior to take away their sin. This was accomplished when Jesus Christ came to earth to live a perfect life and, by that obedience, was able to be the sacrifice to satisfy God's wrath for all who believe.

The deity of Christ and the amazing plan that was set forth before the foundation of the earth is the core of Christian doctrine. The earthly life of Jesus was the fulfillment of many prophecies and confirms the truthfulness of the Bible. His miracles and presence in human form demonstrate that God is both intimately concerned with His creation and able to control it in an absolute way.

Other contexts include:

Psychology—popular secular psychology teaches of the inherent goodness of man, but Christ has lived the only perfect life. Mankind needs a Savior to redeem it from its unrighteousness.

Biology—Christ's virgin birth demonstrates God's sovereignty over nature.

Physics—turning the water into wine and the feeding of the five thousand demonstrate Christ's deity and His sovereignty over nature.

History—time is marked (in the western world) based on the birth of Christ despite current efforts to change the meaning.

Art—much art is based on the life of Christ and many of the masters are known for these depictions, whether on canvas or in music.

Cross

Because God is perfectly just and holy, He must punish sin. The sinless life of Jesus Christ was offered as a substitutionary sacrifice for all of those who will repent and put their faith in the Savior. After His death on the Cross, He defeated death by rising on the third day and is now seated at the right hand of God.

The events surrounding the crucifixion and resurrection have a most significant place in the life of Christians. Though there is no way to scientifically prove the resurrection, there is likewise no way to prove the stories of evolutionary history. These are matters of faith founded in the truth of God's Word and His character. The eyewitness testimony of over 500 people and the written Word of God provide the basis for our belief.

Other contexts include:

Biology—the biological details of the crucifixion can be studied alongside the anatomy of the human body.

History—the use of crucifixion as a method of punishment was short-lived in historical terms and not known at the time it was prophesied.

Art—the crucifixion and resurrection have inspired many wonderful works of art.

Consummation

God, in His great mercy, has promised that He will restore the earth to its original state—a world without death, suffering, war, and disease. The corruption introduced by Adam's sin will be removed. Those who have repented and put their trust in the completed work of Christ on the Cross will experience life in this new heaven and earth. We will be able to enjoy and worship God forever in a perfect place.

This future event is a little more difficult to connect with academic subjects. However, the hope of a life in God's presence and in the absence of sin can be inserted in discussions of human conflict, disease, suffering, and sin in general.

Other contexts include:

History—in discussions of war or human conflict the coming age offers hope.

Biology—the violent struggle for life seen in the predator-prey relationships will no longer taint the earth.

Medicine—while we struggle to find cures for diseases and alleviate the suffering of those enduring the effects of the Curse, we ultimately place our hope in the healing that will come in the eternal state.

The preceding examples are given to provide ideas for integrating the Seven C's of History into a broad range of curriculum activities. We would recommend that you give your students, and yourself, a better understanding of the Seven C's framework by presenting lessons on the Seven C'sfrom AiG's *Answers for Kids* curriculum. This curriculum begins with seven lessons that will establish a solid understanding of the true history, and future, of the universe. Full lesson plans, activities, and student resources are provided in the curriculum set. See www.AnswersBookstore.com to order.

We also offer bookmarks displaying the Seven C's and a wall chart. These can be used as visual cues for the students to help them recall the information and integrate new learning into its proper place in a biblical worldview.

Even if you use other curricula, you can still incorporate the Seven C's teaching into those. Using this approach will help students make firm connections between biblical events and every aspect of the world around them, and they will begin to develop a truly biblical worldview and not just add pieces of the Bible to what they learn in "the real world."

Resources for the teacher

- A teacher's guide is included for each lesson. This guide was written for a 45-minute Sunday school program, taught once a week for a school year (34 weeks). The student lessons are intended for completion during the class period, with no home assignments. However, the lesson usually has more content than can be completed thoroughly in one Sunday school period. Opportunities are therefore available to extend the lesson an extra week in some cases, as well as to give homework assignments if desired. The lessons can also be adapted for daily use in a Christian school or homeschool environment.
- Appendix materials are included for many lessons on a separate CD. These include masters that you can use in PowerPoint, transparencies or printouts.
- This course is built on the Precept Upon Precept courses for Genesis part 1 and 2, written by Kay Arthur, Sheila Richardson and Dr. Kurt Wise. It would be extremely helpful for you as a teacher to work through these courses prior to teaching this class. Videos with lectures by Dr. Wise are available for each lesson and are useful supplementary materials.
- Other supplementary materials are available at www.AnswersInGenesis.org.

It All Begins With Genesis

LESSON 1

There is more than one way to look at your world

Scripture: Genesis 1:1, 26, 31

Psalm 148:5; Isaiah 40:26; 45:12; Colossians 1:16 (Creator)
2 Timothy 3:16; Psalm 119:142; John 1:14; 14:6; 17:17 (authority of Scripture)

Suggested memory verse (choose one): Colossians 1:16; 2 Timothy 3:16; John 17:17

What this lesson is about:

This lesson introduces the term 'worldview.' It points to Scripture as the eyewitness to the origin of all things, and it addresses Scripture's claim to absolute truth.

7 C's Connection: Creation

Goals for the lesson: The student should

- be able to define 'worldview.'
- understand the importance of the eyewitness (Scripture).
- see Scripture's claim to truth.
- see what the eyewitness of Scripture claims regarding the creation of all things.

Preparation for lesson:

- Work through student's lesson 1.
- Read through the 'delicious cake mystery' (page T-13). Provide cake and the players necessary to perform the skit.
- Prepare word puzzle materials (page T-15). You will also need glue or tape.
- Funny eyeglasses (one pair for biblical worldview and one for naturalistic worldview) are helpful in illustrations.

Plan for lesson:

- Begin with the 'delicious cake mystery' illustration (page T-13). The students should see that there is usually more than one reasonable explanation of the data (facts), yet two different explanations can't both be true. The eyewitness report can often settle the matter.
- Apply this principle to the creation of the world. Help students see the two major explanations that people have for the data. Ask, 'Are both reasonable?' *(yes)* 'Can both be true?' *(no)* Ask, 'What is the eyewitness?' *(Scripture)*

- Apply also to the creation of man. Let students see the two ways that the origin of man is explained—ask the same questions.
- Use this discussion as a springboard to introduce the concept of 'worldview.' Give out word puzzle pieces (found on page T-15—reproduce as necessary) and ask students to arrange them to form a definition for worldview. (Correct definition: 'A total way of looking at the world' or 'A way of looking at the total world.') When they have glued the definition into their notebooks, discuss the other definitions given in the lesson and discuss the big questions that a worldview answers. Tell students that your goal this year will be to develop a biblical worldview, with answers to all of these questions. You will also look at the other major way of looking at the world: the naturalistic worldview. (If you have two different pairs of eyeglasses, you can use them to illustrate the two different views.) Students will see which view is the most compelling and evaluate where truth lies.
- **Class work.** Ask, 'What about this eyewitness, the Bible? Can it be trusted? How can we know what is really true?' Have the students work through the five cross-references given in their lesson. Discuss their answers. (You can do this all together by having a student read the verse aloud and everyone discussing the answer.)
- **Class work.** Now look at the next group of cross-references. They give the biblical worldview for how all things came to be. Have the students go through the Scriptures and instruct them to highlight or underline what the eyewitness teaches about the origin of all things. (You can have them work on their own or you can work together.)
- Conclude by discussing the final questions: Does it make a difference? How can it change what you think and how you live?

If you have additional time . . .
Suggestions for augmenting lessons (home school, day school)

This lesson introduces the concept of worldviews. These are abstract concepts and will require frequent reinforcement. It would be helpful to add one more session to this lesson. It would allow more time to study the cross-references. It would also allow expanded illustration concerning what makes up a worldview.

Activity: The Delicious Cake Mystery

This activity addresses the question 'How can we *know* what is true?' Children experience this confusion when they are taught biblical principles in the home and then hear conflicting ideas outside the home. They hear opposing sides to an issue, and both seem reasonable. It is never too early to begin to teach children to question, to discern, to realize that someone who seems smart may not necessarily be speaking truth. This realization will lead into an understanding of 'worldviews,' which is a difficult concept for both children and adults to work into their thinking, but it is most valuable. Worldviews will be addressed at length as this course continues. The key thought to communicate in this activity is that the Bible contains absolute truth, and it is the only eyewitness report about the Creation. It must be the foundation on which we build all scientific models and answer all questions to which it speaks.

Materials needed:

A cake. (the more decorated and enticing, the better!)

Three actors. (Prompt three students before the class, or enlist helpers. For the complete conversation, see 'Procedure' on the next page.)

1. One will say the name of the person he thinks made the cake. (It could be the mother, the teacher or someone else whom everyone knows.)
2. The second will say, 'No, she bought it at the bakery.'
   The problem: 'Which is true?'
3. The third will stay outside the room until the discussion of the clues (below) has finished, and will come in and reveal that he was the eyewitness, who clinches the solution to the mystery.

   (Because of time constraints, you can perform one part and enlist another teacher or helper to play the other two parts.)

3x5 index cards. On each card, write a clue. (Or you can skip the cards and simply carry on a dialogue with the other teacher or helper.) You can make up your own clues, but some suggestions include the following:

[Name of the suspected cake maker] loves to cook, and she often bakes cakes.
The bakery near you home had a special sale on cakes today.
There was a mixing bowl and spoons and a pan in the dishwasher this morning.
This cake is more beautiful than the cakes she usually makes.
She has recently taken a cake-decorating course.
Ten dollars is missing from her wallet.
The flour canister is empty and some flour has been spilled on the floor.
Jerry saw her in town this afternoon, only two blocks from the bakery.
You saw a cake in the bakery yesterday that looked like this cake.

Procedure: (Note: The italic type represents what the parent or teacher may want to say to the class by way of explanation. You may simply read this to the class or rephrase it in your own words and add other explanatory information.)

1. (Present the cake to the group to admire.) *Look what I just found! Isn't it a beautiful cake? Who made this cake—does anyone know?* One student (prompted earlier by you) will say the name of someone who may have made the cake. Another will say the cake was bought at the bakery.
2. *How do we know which is true? Are there any clues?* (Pick up the stack of index cards with the clues on them.) *Scientists would call this 'data.' What observations can we conclude about this situation from these clue cards?*
3. Go through the index cards with the clues on them. Ask the class to say which hypothesis each clue card favors. Keep score on the board.
4. *Well, we've gone through both sets of cards and made our observations. Both choices seem plausible. How can we know?* Now your final 'planted' actor comes into the room and announces to the person who allegedly made the cake, 'It was great seeing you this afternoon when you came into the bakery and bought that yummy-looking cake. I came over for a piece of that cake.'
5. Ask them, *What is so important about this last development?* They should see that an eyewitness report (if it is a credible eyewitness) is much more valuable than a bunch of clues that can be interpreted in different ways.
6. Ask them, *What does this have to do with the creation of the world?* (Give them a chance to answer.) *When it comes to the creation of the world, we often hear more than one idea about how it happened.* (You can let them tell you what they have heard—the two basic views are that God created the world or it happened by chance through evolution.) *There is more than one story of how things got here, and each has evidence you can see, and each can be pretty persuasive. But was there an eyewitness to Creation?* (They should be able to tell you that only God would know, and He told us in the Bible.) *The only eyewitness report is found in the Bible. That should be our final evaluation of what is true. The truth is found in God's Word. It is the only truth that is fully reliable. It should settle the mystery of how the world and all that is in it came to be.*

You can then eat the cake for snack time!

Worldview puzzle template*

A	WAY	OF	LOOKING
AT	THE	TOTAL	WORLD

A	WAY	OF	LOOKING
AT	THE	TOTAL	WORLD

A	WAY	OF	LOOKING
AT	THE	TOTAL	WORLD

A	WAY	OF	LOOKING
AT	THE	TOTAL	WORLD

A	WAY	OF	LOOKING
AT	THE	TOTAL	WORLD

*This activity is used by permission of Summit Ministries, found in their curriculum *Worldviews in Focus: Thinking like a Christian* by David Noebel and Chuck Edwards, Summit Ministries, 1999. Summit Press, PO Box 207, Manitou Springs, Colorado 80829.

It All Begins With Genesis

LESSON 2

The foundation for your worldview is Genesis

Scripture: Psalm 11:3; selected passages from Genesis 3–11

Suggested memory verse (choose one): Psalm 11:3; Genesis 1:1

What this lesson is about:

This lesson teaches that Genesis is the foundation for the biblical worldview. When a foundation is destroyed, the entire building tumbles. The lesson also introduces the inductive study principle of the overview, and leads the students in a simple overview of Genesis 1–11.

7C's Connection: Creation, Corruption, Catastrophe, Confusion

Goals for the lesson: The student should

- be able to give a definition of 'worldview.'
- have a beginning understanding of foundations and why Genesis is foundational.
- know the four main events of Genesis 1–11.

Preparation for lesson:

- Work through the student's lesson 2.
- Prepare a bulletin board with the information about worldviews presented in last week's lesson. (You could include definitions given in the lesson, worldview questions and pictures of many different people looking at the world.)
- 'Props' for lesson: building blocks and toy house, toy helicopter or photograph of flyover view and toy eyeglasses with different colors of 'glass.'

Plan for lesson:

- **Review** last's week concept of *worldviews.* Give out the toy eyeglasses and ask the students what color different objects appear to be. After they 'see' different colors, use this as a springboard to talk about the worldview lesson from last week. Use the bulletin board to review the definition of worldview and the kind of questions answered by the worldview.
- Tell the students that they will be studying Genesis this year, because Genesis is the foundation of the biblical worldview. You might illustrate the foundational nature of Genesis by using building blocks and a toy house. Have a house perched on a big foundation and then invite a student to knock out the foundation from underneath.

- Ask students if they know why Genesis is called the *foundation* of Scripture. If they can't tell you, wait until they have finished their class work and then discuss it with them. Discuss Psalm 11:3 and ask them about the consequences of having a foundation removed.
- Tell your students that they will be learning *inductive Bible study* while they study Genesis. They will learn all about what 'inductive' actually means next week, but today they will begin by doing the first step of inductive study.
- Explain what an *overview* is and why it is necessary when you study Scripture. An overview is like flying over something in a helicopter—it gives you the 'big picture' and helps you to see how the different pieces all fit together. If you have an aerial photograph, you can show how the overview enables you to see what is there and how things fit together. They need to see how they can't see all of those things from the ground perspective.
- **Class work.** Show the students the chart that they need to complete (on page 9 of their workbooks), and tell them that they are to look for the four main events of the first 11 chapters of Genesis. Let them look up the Scriptures in their Bibles and fill in the chart. Then they can draw a picture to represent each event. The four major events they should identify: the Creation, the Flood, the Fall, the nations. (Depending upon your time and number of students involved, you may wish to assign one verse for each student to look up and read as you prompt them. The group as a whole can identify the event being described.)
- **Discussion.** Look at each major event described in Genesis and ask the students how these things could be explained if they didn't have Genesis.

  Chapters 1–2 (Creation of all things, establishment of marriage, man's dominion over earth) If we had no Genesis, we would have to explain creation with some kind of evolutionary scenario, marriage would not necessarily be between a man and a woman (homosexuality, no covenantal marriage, etc.), and man would be on same level as animals ('animal rights').

  Chapters 3–5 (The Fall of mankind, results of the Fall—including murder and death) If we had no Genesis, we would have no way to explain death, pain, sorrow, evil, thorns and thistles in the world.

  Chapters 6–9 (The Flood) If we had no Genesis, then billions of fossils deposited in the Flood would have to be explained naturalistically, we would not understand God as a Judge, and we would underestimate the power of God.

  Chapters 10–11 (Babel, descendants of the sons of Noah, origin of languages and nations) If we had no Genesis, we would not know the origin of people groups and languages; some people would consider racism justifiable.

If you have additional time . . .
Suggestions for augmenting lessons (home school, day school)

Suggested addition: five more sessions

It would be helpful to do a complete overview of Genesis 1–11, if you have the time. Using the student observation sheets, instruct students to read each chapter and pick out the *who* (people in the chapter), *what* (events in the chapter) and *where* (geographical allusions) of each chapter. Then summarize the theme of each chapter and draw a picture of the main event in the chapter.

You could break it down:

Session 1: chapters 1–2
Session 2: chapters 3–5
Session 3: chapters 6–8
Session 4: chapters 9–11
Session 5: summary and review

Ask the students what would be missing from our understanding of our faith if we didn't have Genesis. Ask them what worldview questions will be answered by studying Genesis. Create a time-line bulletin board.

Older students would probably benefit from watching Dr. Kurt Wise's video lesson 1 from the adult Precept course Genesis 1.

Other valuable resources include Ken Ham's talk 'Is Genesis relevant today?' (a 30-minute video in the seminar series *Answers ... with Ken Ham*) and *Demolishing Strongholds* sessions 1 and 2, available on DVD from www.AnswersInGenesis.org.

It All Begins With Genesis

LESSON 3

Inductive Bible study: We learn to observe

Scripture: Genesis 1:1–31

Suggested memory verse (choose one):

Genesis 1:1; 1:31

What this lesson is about:

This lesson teaches basic principles of inductive Bible study: *Five W's and H.* Students will learn truths from Genesis 1 by making notes on a special 'observation worksheet.'

7 C's Connection: Creation, Corruption, Catastrophe

Goals for the lesson: The student should

- know the definition of inductive Bible study.
- know the three components of inductive Bible study (observation, interpretation, application).
- be able to read simple verses and tell what questions are being answered in the verse (Five W's and H).
- remember the four main events of Genesis.
- begin to learn how to 'read with a purpose' as the student searches for the words 'God' and 'man' in Genesis 1.

Preparation for lesson:

- Work through student's lesson 3.
- Begin time-line bulletin board (page T-24). Provide bulletin-board paper and signs for the four events of Genesis 1–11.
- Illustration for Genesis 1 and markers.
- Students will need their observation sheet for Genesis 1. Colored pens, pencils or highlighters are also needed.
- Begin the Inductive Bible Study bulletin board. Include definitions, three components, six magic words and the first two steps of inductive study. (More detailed instructions are in the 'Plan for lesson' on the next page.) *Eleven* visuals for this lesson are on the CD that comes with this curriculum.

Plan for lesson:

- **Review.** Ask your students if they remember what part of inductive study you began last week (the overview) and the four major events of Genesis discovered from that overview. (This is a good time to begin a time line of history. See directions for a time-line activity at the end of this lesson.) Before the students arrive, you could prepare the wall with a long sheet of bulletin-board paper. As they respond to your questions about the four events of Genesis, place signs depicting Creation, the Fall, the Flood and the nations at appropriate places on the paper. Tell students that they will be filling in the details in the weeks to come.)
- Include some formal teaching on 'What is inductive study?' This topic is included in their lesson. They need to understand the definition of 'inductive study,' the three components of inductive study and the 'magic words' of the Five W's and H. (Suggestion: Prepare your wall for another visual aid. You could title the space 'What is inductive Bible study?' As you teach, place visuals on the board. Include the definition of inductive study, the three components of inductive study and the six magic words. You will add to this bulletin board as new principles of study are introduced later in the lesson and in future weeks. Several visuals are available on the CD that came with this curriculum.)
- Teach the 'magic words' of inductive Bible study. You can use many 'down home' illustrations, such as in the game of Jeopardy, where the answer is given and the contestant has to respond by telling what the question is. You could have a simple game with everyday questions and answers. For example:

'The church we go to.'	**'What' is Trinity?**
'The place where my sister goes to college.'	**'Where' is UCLA?**
'The celebration of Jesus' birthday.'	**'When' is December 25?**

- Next you could use three Genesis cross-references (1:1; 2:8; 3:10) to see if students can tell you what questions are answered by the verses. (Genesis 1:1 answers *when, who did what;* Genesis 2:8 tells you *who did what, where;* Genesis 3:10 tells you *who did what, why* and *what*)
- Teach next the second step of inductive Bible study as you prepare students for group work. Ask them to tell you the first step—the one they did last week (the overview). (If you are working on a bulletin board for inductive study, add 'The Four Steps of Inductive Study' and then 'Step One: The Overview ... Helicopter View.') Then teach them 'Step Two: Hiking.' In the second step they will study Genesis 1 in more detail.
- **Class work.** Refer students to the observation sheet for Genesis 1 found in their books.

    1. Today they will begin by marking 'God.' Be sure to include all the pronouns and any other names of God.

       Emphasize that each time they mark a word, students should think about what question is being answered. When they finish marking 'God,' ask them briefly something they learned about God as a result of marking His name. (This will be done in detail in next week's lesson.)

2. Next, have them mark 'man' and other synonyms and pronouns.
3. If time permits, list in the margin what was created on each Day of Creation Week.
4. Again, if time permits, refer them to the theme of Genesis 1 at the end of their observation sheet. Teach them that a theme is what is talked about the most, the main topic of the chapter. Have them circle the best theme and draw a picture of the events of the chapter.

Suggested illustrations and activities:

- Begin the historical time-line bulletin board. Add the four major events of Genesis.
- Play a game of Jeopardy in order to teach how to think in 'who, what, where, when, why and how' kinds of questions.
- Begin the Inductive Bible Study bulletin board. Add visuals for each principle (as you teach it).

  Note to teacher: This is a *lot* of material for one lesson—challenging even for adults. New concepts are introduced and new tools are being taught. Be realistic in your expectations for the students. This is just the beginning. You will be repeating these principles, and students will be practicing the tools over and over. You have just begun! Keep up your enthusiasm and encourage your students for the start they have made. The Lord is pleased when we seek to study His Word in depth, and He will reward us with understanding.

If you have additional time . . .
Suggestions for augmenting lessons (home school, day school)

Suggested addition: two more sessions

These early lessons introduce new concepts in every lesson, and additional time to discuss and practice the tools taught would be very helpful. One or two additional sessions would allow you to include more illustration and practice in learning to observe, to interpret and apply biblical passages, and to practice asking the Five W's and H. Use other familiar verses from the Bible for the exercises.

The lesson suggests a beginning 'observation' of Genesis 1. This could take one full session.

Since this is the first time students are asked to mark key words, it is probably good to use a transparency and go through the process with them.

Activity: time line

Time lines can be excellent tools to help students to remember the events in Genesis. This time line will eventually cover everything from Creation to Abraham. You will begin the time line this week and then add to it as the course progresses. The activity is designed so that every student can add something to it, so use as big a wall as possible for the project. The more the class can add to it, the more they'll remember and the more fun you'll have. (Note: If it is impossible to find space for one big time line, you can make individual time lines. For example, the activity for this week would be simply to make a time line for the four main events of Genesis 1–11.)

Materials needed:

Wall space. (Take as much as possible.)

Paper. (The best paper for a time line can be bought at a teacher's supply store. Purchase the rolls of paper that are used to cover bulletin boards. The paper is approximately 30 inches in height and gives plenty of room for the project. You can buy it by the roll or sometimes by the foot, in a variety of colors.)

Paper, magazines, crayons, markers, scissors. These are to be used for various additions to the time line.

Procedure:

1. Your time line should be anywhere from 8 to 12 ft long (longer if you have over 20 children) so that you will have lots of room for class contributions. (If you are doing a time line for your family, you can make it smaller, around 6 ft.)
2. Cut the appropriate length of paper and lightly mark off four equal lengths at the bottom of the paper. These will be reference points for the different events that you'll record as you complete the study. Hang the time line on the wall.
3. You may wish to place the key time markers on the time line, in order to allow room for things that are coming and to see the 'big picture':

   First quarter of time line: Creation Week
   Second quarter of time line: Creation to the Fall
   Third quarter of time line: The Fall to the Flood
   Fourth quarter of time line: The Flood to Abraham

4. For this lesson, prepare your overview collage. If the time line is for a class, divide the class into four groups. Have each group draw one of the major events. You can give each group a large piece of paper to work on together, or you can give each member a small piece of paper (one-half or one-fourth of a blank 8.5 x 11 sheet of paper). Place the pictures within each major event division. As the study progresses, the students will continue to add to the time line.

It All Begins With Genesis

LESSON 4

Hiking through Genesis 1

Scripture: Genesis 1:1–31

Suggested Memory Verse (choose one):

Genesis 1:1; 1:31

What this lesson is about:

This lesson continues to teach the basic principles of inductive Bible study: the *Five W's and H. Key Words* are introduced, and the process of observing a chapter is continued. The character of God is the focus of this first chapter of Genesis.

7 C's Connection: Creation

Goals for the lesson: The student should

- learn the definition of a key word.
- have a beginning understanding of the process of 'observing' a chapter.
- know the basic events of Genesis 1.
- be able to express something he has learned about God the Creator.

Preparation for lesson:

- Work through student's lesson 4.
- Prepare a 'key' illustration and definition of key words to add to the Inductive Bible Study bulletin board.
- Use the observation sheet for Genesis 1 to illustrate how to mark key words.

Plan for lesson:

- Review the first two steps of inductive study introduced last week. (You could cover up the steps that you placed on the Inductive Bible Study bulletin board last week, and ask students to tell you what they are.)
- Ask the students to take out their observation sheets for chapter 1 begun last week. Review the principles of finding truth from Scripture by asking the 'Five W's and H' questions about the text. You might 'test' students by giving some simple verses.

- Teach the definition of key words. Ask students to tell you what key words they marked on their observation sheets last week.
- Be sure you go through all the instructions before students start their class work. They need to understand
  1. how to mark a key word and different ways to mark them. (At this point in their learning process, it is probably best to tell them how to mark each word. Illustrate marking 'God' on an overhead transparency of the observation sheet for Genesis 1.)
  2. that synonyms of the word are also marked in the same way (e.g. different names for God have the same marking). Be sure students know what 'synonym' means. (Illustrate using the Genesis 1 observation sheet.)
  3. that pronouns of the key words must be marked as well. (Illustrate using the Genesis 1 observation sheet.)
- **Class work.** Review worksheets from last week to be sure students marked all the references to God (purple crown) and to man (blue stick figure for generic man; pink stick figure when woman is specified.)
- **Class work.** Mark every mention of 'said' by drawing a red box around the word. Ask students what they learned about 'said.' What is the connection between the Lord speaking and things happening? Draw their attention to Psalm 33:6 in their lesson. Ask what they learned from Psalm 33:6 when the Lord spoke.
- **Class work.** Ask if they saw any other 'action verbs'—other things God 'did' in addition to 'saying.' Have students mark the remaining verbs by drawing a black box around them (created, saw, separated, called, made, placed, blessed).
- **Key phrases class work.** After they finish marking the key verbs, prepare students for the last assignment of the day: key phrases. Ask them what a phrase is, and see if they can identify some repeated phrases in chapter 1. Instruct them to mark the following phrases on their observation sheets:

<It was good.> (blue brackets)
<It was so.> (orange brackets)
<After their [or its] kind.> (green brackets)

- **Closing discussion**. Discuss what students learned about the character of God from the key words marked. It would be helpful to make a list on the board of things they learn about God as they give them to you.

  Ask them what they learned about God from the action words (verbs).

  Some things they may see from the various verbs:

  'created' = all the variety of what He created, power to create it all from nothing, intelligence
  'said' = intent, command, power, attention to detail, diversity. When God speaks something into existence, it happens.
  'saw' = love and care, beauty, order
  'separated' = God makes distinctions.
  'called' = sovereignty
  'made' = beauty, intelligence
  'blessed' = God's love

Suggested illustrations and activities:

- Ask students to help you make a list of the truths they learn about God from marking the key words and phrases. Use a visual aid, such as a white board, flip chart or poster paper.
- Use an overhead transparency to llustrate how to mark the observation sheet.
- Assign the activity of observing the universe on a clear night and making a list about what you learn about God from the universe.

If you have additional time . . .
Suggestions for augmenting lessons (home school, day school)

Suggested addition: one or two more sessions

One or two more sessions would be helpful both to master the mechanics of marking key words and phrases and to have a more thorough discussion of what students learn about God through the verbs and phrases of chapter 1.

You will need to reinforce the concept of worldviews continually and the need to answer the question 'Who is God?' as you study this chapter.

If you are integrating this lesson with physical science or life science, an excellent video to add is lesson 1 by Dr Kurt Wise, found in part 1 of Precept's *Genesis* course. It contains some more advanced scientific concepts, but it pulls together the answer to 'Who is God?' beautifully.

It All Begins With Genesis

LESSON 5

The Trinity in Creation

Scripture: Genesis 1; Colossians 1:15–16; Hebrews 1:1–2, Hebrews 11:3

Suggested memory verse (choose one):

Colossians 1:15–16; Hebrews 11:3

What this lesson is about:

This lesson addresses the worldview question 'Who is God?' by looking at the role of the Trinity in creation. It also introduces steps 3 and 4 of the four-step inductive study process: *word studies* and *cross-references.* It concludes with continued 'observation' of chapter 1 and the Days of Creation.

7 C's Connection: Creation

Goals for the lesson: The student should

- be able to list the four steps of the inductive study process.
- know what a cross-reference is.
- be able to explain what the Trinity is and how each member of the Trinity was involved in creation.
- be able to express something he has learned about God from studying the role of the Trinity in creation.
- begin to learn the events of each Day of Creation.

Preparation for lesson:

- Work through student's lesson 5.
- Paper and tape to cover some of the inductive bulletin board signs.
- Two signs for the inductive bulletin board: step 3 'Smell the roses' and step 4 'Satellite view.'
- Additional signs for the inductive bulletin board, showing Hebrew words (if possible, include actual Hebrew letters, found in most concordances): *Elohim, Jehovah, El Elyon, rahap.*

Plan for lesson:

- **Review time!** Direct the students to the first page of today's lesson. Give them five minutes to write what each of the icons represents concerning inductive study. (If you have an inductive study bulletin board in the room, cover up the answers to the questions before the class arrives.)

- Teach step 3 of inductive study: 'Stop and smell the roses.' Continue the analogy of the view from the helicopter (the overview of the four events of Genesis 1–11), and the hiking view (the key words that students marked in chapter 1). Now it is time to get even closer: see the flowers, rocks and other little details that they find on the 'hike.' The corresponding step in Bible study is to look at the meaning of the Hebrew or Greek words. (Put up a sign saying, 'Step 3: Stop and smell the roses. Word Studies' on your ongoing inductive study bulletin board.)
- Introduce Hebrew words. Explain that the Old Testament was written in Hebrew and the New Testament in Greek. It would be helpful if you could have a poster that includes something written in the actual language. Then write the word '*Elohim*' on the board. Tell the students that '*Elohim*' is what is called a 'transliteration' of the actual Hebrew word. Discuss what the lesson says about the meaning of this particular name of God. It would also be helpful to illustrate how the names used for God serve to teach something about His character. For example, you could include the example of Jehovah (YHWH) to illustrate the covenant name for God, and *El Elyon* as an example of the Most High, Sovereign God.
- Ask, 'What is the Trinity?' See what their understanding is of this doctrinal truth. Inform them that *Elohim* is a plural noun that is used with a singular verb (be sure they know what singular and plural mean). Ask if anyone can tell you how the use of *Elohim* in the plural tells you about the God who was there at creation? (This is a possible reference to the entire Trinity being involved in the creation process.) Instruct them to write the answer in the space given on the top of page 27 of their lesson.
- Tell them that we now need to find out more about what role the different members of the Trinity played in creation. Direct them to Genesis 1:2, written in their lesson (God the Holy Spirit), and take them through the questions answered by that verse. Give them time to write the answers in their lesson.
- Another word study is related to Genesis 1:3. Write on the board or put up a sign with the Hebrew '*rahap*' and its meaning 'flutter or vibrate.' Discuss how vibrations lead to energy. (Ask them to rub their hands together and feel the heat—a kind of energy.) Direct them next to Genesis 1:3 and ask them to write what happened after the Spirit began 'vibrating' (light—a form of energy).
- **Class work.** The lesson includes three cross-references from Colossians and Hebrews. Instruct students to read them and answer the who, what, where, when, why and how questions. If time permits and they seem to understand the process, allow them to do the work themselves. If you do not have time for individual work, you can take them through the exercise step by step.
- **Discussion.** (It would be helpful to write the students' answers on the board as they give them to you.)

  Ask, 'What was the Holy Spirit's role at Creation?' *(He moved over the water, and then there was light. The Spirit of God had an energizing role in creation, Genesis 1:2.)*

Ask, 'What was Jesus' role at Creation?' *(Jesus created all things. He is also the Sustainer of creation. All things were created by Him and for Him, Colossians 1:15–16.)*

Ask, 'What was God the Father's role at Creation?' *(Through Jesus Christ, God made the world, according to Hebrews 1:2. The universe was formed by the Word of God. God is the Designer/Planner of creation; by His will it was created, according to Hebrews 11:3.)*

Ask, 'What do you learn about God from all this? What difference should it make in your life?

- Show students how they have just completed step 4 of inductive study. Ask them if they know what a 'cross-reference' is. Explain how cross-references help us understand what we are studying in a deeper way. (Put up the step 4 sign 'Satellite view' on your ongoing inductive study bulletin board.)
- **Class work.** 'Six Days of Creation' chart

  Have students go back to their observation worksheet for chapter 1 and use it to fill out the chart on page 31 of their lesson. Inform them that you will begin their next lesson with an activity that will test how well they know what happened on each Day of Creation.

If you have additional time . . .
Suggestions for augmenting lessons (home school, day school)

Three more sessions could be effectively added to this lesson—a total of four sessions to cover the content of the lesson.

The first session could focus on the mechanics of the fours steps of inductive study.

The second session could teach word studies using a concordance. Show students how to find the Hebrew transliteration of a word.

The third session could focus on the Trinity, using both cross-references and word study.

The fourth session could involve making a chart of the events of the Days of Creation and reviewing all the new tools learned.

Answers in Genesis has several valuable resources to augment classroom discussion, including Ken Ham's talk 'Did God Create in Six Literal Days?' (a 30-minute video in the 12-segment seminar series *Answers ... with Ken Ham,* available on DVD from www.AnswersInGenesis.org).

The Days of Creation: A closer look at Days 1-3

Scripture: Genesis 1:1–31

Suggested memory verse: Any verse from Genesis 1

What this lesson is about:

This lesson looks closely at Days 1–3 of Creation, encouraging the student to visualize what the Bible teaches about the events of each Day. It addresses the meaning of key phrases, such as 'formless and void,' 'the expanse' and 'after their kind.' Students will be asked to draw pictures of each Day of Creation.

7 C's Connection: Creation

Goals for the lesson: The student should

- know what happened on each of the first three Days of Creation.
- understand these events as biblical truth, not myth.
- have an increased sense of awe and wonder at the God of Creation by thinking through what He made.
- think. In many cases the complete answers are not available, but students should be excited about considering the wonder of the creation, and enjoy the mind that God has given them.

Preparation for lesson:

- Work through student's lesson 6.
- Assemble 'props' for the lesson:

Sign with Hebrew word *raqia* (expanse) for the inductive bulletin board
Last week's sign with the Hebrew word *rahap* (moving)
Clippings for the Days of Creation treasure hunt (T-37) or 'silent unscramble' (T-38; you may wish to bring candy or some simple prizes for the winners.)
Blender, biscuit and water for the Day 1 illustration (see T-36)
Paper and markers to draw Days of Creation for the time-line bulletin board

Plan for lesson:

- **Introduction.** Ask the students to think about what it would be like to be a spectator sitting in the grandstands watching God create the universe and all that is. Wow!

Ask them if they know why it is important to learn the Days of Creation.

Ask, 'What's wrong with saying, "All that matters is that God created the heavens and the earth—all the details aren't really necessary." ' (Answers might include the fact that when God speaks, it is important. Therefore, every word of Genesis 1 is vital. In addition, knowing about how He created teaches us more about the character of our God, and it creates a sense of awe and wonder that helps us to know and worship Him better. Also, some may point out that knowing what Scripture actually says about the Creation Days will help them evaluate what they are taught in other places about the origin of the world. They will be better able to discern truth from error.)

- **Review.** Instruct the students to take out the chart of the Days of Creation found at the end of lesson 5. Go through the general day-by-day events to check their answers.
- **Activities.** The 'Days of Creation treasure hunt' is an excellent way to practice learning the events of the Creation Days. This works well if your group is small and you have a lot of space to move around. However, if your group is large and space limited, the 'Days of Creation silent unscramble' can be substituted effectively. (Directions for these activities are found at the end of this lesson.)
- **Teaching: Day 1 of Creation.** Encourage your class to picture what was happening. God created the heavens and earth 'without form.' The biscuit illustration (activity at the end of this lesson) may help them visualize this point. You next can show the sign from last week's lesson about the Holy Spirit's 'hovering' *(rahap)* over the waters, and ask what happens when a vibrating motion takes place. (When the Holy Spirit 'fluttered' or 'moved' over the surface of the waters, the forces were introduced.)
- **Class work.** Have students draw the events of Day 1 of Creation. (You might find it helpful to ask some of the students to make their drawings on larger paper. Their drawings can be posted on the Genesis time-line bulletin board, begun a few weeks ago.)
- **Teaching: Day 2 of Creation.** Ask students to put their observation sheets for chapter 1 in front of them. Introduce the word 'expanse' *(raqia)* with a word-study sign, which you will then place on the inductive Bible study bulletin board under step 4 'Word studies.'

Explain that we need to understand precisely what God means by 'expanse.' Take students through the exercise on page 35 of their lesson, having them define 'expanse' by looking first at verses 7–8, then at verses 16–17 and finally at verse 20. Then ask where, in the light of Scripture, the 'waters above' are located. (Genesis 1:8 indicates that the expanse is a place separated by waters above and below.)

In 1:14, we see that the sun, moon and stars are located in the expanse; therefore, the entire universe is between the waters above and below. Hmmm ... it seems to be describing a water boundary to the known universe—something we can't see at this point.

In 1:20 we see that the birds fly 'across' the expanse; therefore, the atmosphere appears to be included in the expanse. (However, it is important to realize that Hebrew prepositions, such as 'above,' 'across' and 'below,' can be flexible in meaning, and so it is difficult to be dogmatic.)

This exercise becomes relevant if you explain the four ways the 'waters above' are interpreted by biblical scholars today. As you go over each interpretation, ask students to evaluate which interpretation seems to be most consistent with their observations about the text.

1. The 'waters above' refer to the clouds in our atmosphere. The 'waters below' refer to the ocean. *(Not biblical if the expanse includes the place where the sun, moon and stars are located.)*

2. The 'waters above' refer to the oceans, while the 'waters below' refer to underground water. *(Not biblical, according to the text's apparent definition of 'expanse.')*

3. The 'waters above' refer to a water vapor canopy above our present atmosphere. This canopy collapsed at the Flood and supplied the necessary water to flood the earth. The 'waters below' are the oceans. *(Not biblical if the expanse includes the sun, moon and stars. The proposed canopy would have to be between the atmosphere—where the birds fly—and the sun, moon and stars. The well-known 'canopy theory' is apparently not biblical, according to the most straightforward definition of 'expanse' in Genesis 1.)*

4. The 'waters above' refer to the boundary of the universe; the 'waters below' refer to the oceans. *(This seems to be what is described in Genesis 1. We could then infer that the known universe is bounded. This goes against any of the evolutionary cosmogonies, which assume the universe has no boundary.)*

- **Class work.** Instruct the students to draw the events of Day 2 of Creation. Post selected drawings on the time-line bulletin board.

- **Teaching: Day 3 of Creation.** Ask the class what happened on Day 3. Then ask them to visualize what happened. (Was water destroyed and land created in its place? Was water changed to land, similar to the water changed to wine at the wedding feast in Cana? Was the water pushed out and the land zapped in to fill the void? Was the land raised and the waters then ran off the land? What does the description in Genesis 1 lead to you think really happened?)

  Ask if the description in Genesis 1 is talking about one continent or many? (This could lead you to mention plate tectonics and the two ways of looking at the separation of the continents: naturalistic (inch by inch over much time) and biblical (catastrophically at the time of the Flood). Tell students they'll study this in more detail when they study the Flood.)

  Ask whether they notice anything interesting about the creation of the trees and other vegetation. (They should see the repeated phrase 'after their kind' and also note the fact that the vegetation was created in a mature state, with fruit and seeds already present.)

- **Class work.** Instruct the students to draw the events of Day 3 of Creation.

There are other activities available if time and weather permit. You probably won't have time. You might suggest the leaf- or flower-collecting exercise to be done at home and reported next week in class.

Activity: Biscuit of Genesis 1

Sometimes it can be hard to visualize just what we think Genesis 1:1–2 means. How could God make the whole universe and have it be formless and void? This is a simple, quick illustration that should let you have a little fun in your study.

You will need:

A biscuit or roll

A blender or food processor

Water and a glass

Procedure:

1. Set out the above items on a table so the whole class can see.
2. Read Genesis 1:1–2 to the class. Ask the class what that passage means. 'Did God make the heavens and earth, but then they got messed up and He had to start over again in verse 3? Did He make the ingredients for the heavens and earth? What happened?'
3. Pour about a cup of water in the bottom of your blender. Then add the biscuit and mix until fully blended. When finished, hold up the mixture for the class to see. Ask, 'What is in this glass?' *(a biscuit)* 'Could you say this biscuit is formless?' *(definitely!)*

   Explain: In Genesis 1, the wording would suggest that God created all the matter in the universe but initially there was no form. Energy would be required to hold it together and give it shape. When the Holy Spirit began moving or vibrating over the surface of the waters, energy was created.

   So, when you try to visualize Genesis 1:1–2, remember what this unformed biscuit looked like.

Days of Creation Treasure Hunt

This activity is a good way to help the class reinforce the memory of what God made on each Day of Creation. It is a little different from some treasure hunts. You will hide pictures or objects from every Day of Creation, but you will call out each Day of Creation separately. The class is allowed to retrieve an item that they find only if it was created on the Day you call out. You'll want a room with many nooks and crannies, or several rooms so that you can spread out and have a good time.

Materials needed:

> **Objects or pictures of objects representing things that were made on each Day of Creation .** Computer clip art works well for this, if you want to collect your own. For instance, for Day 1 you might cut out pictures of light bulbs or lamps. Day 2 pictures could include clouds, diagrams of the atmosphere, water and open sky. You may get an actual leaf for Day 3. For Day 7, you may want to hide a mini-pillow or a picture of a bed (for 'rest'). Pull together as many objects or pictures as you can for each Day. Be creative. If you wish, you could have the children help you pick out or draw the objects that will be used.

Procedure:

1. Determine if you have enough pictures or objects for each person to find. You will want each person in your class to have a chance to find something that you've hidden for each Day. If you have more children than objects, you may want to group the class into pairs or teams. (Dividing into teams is a great idea, anyway, if you have a wide age range within the class. If you group an older child with a younger, the younger won't have to worry about not finding something.)
2. Explain to the class that they will be going on a Days of Creation hunt. Make sure they understand that they can bring back an object only if it was created on the Day you call out. If they bring back something from a different Day, it will have to be returned. By this time they should be familiar with the Days of Creation, but they can look in the Bible or refer to their lesson if necessary.
3. Call out the Days of Creation in whatever order you wish.
4. When you are finished with the activity, review again what God created on each Day.

Days of Creation Silent Unscramble (Alternate activity if you have a large group)

1. Divide the group into teams.
2. Use the collected clip art drawings (same as for the treasure hunt) and have one complete set for each team. Thoroughly mix up the pictures.
3. Make index cards with numbers from 1 to 7 and place them across a table surface for each team.
4. Instruct the teams to arrange the pile of drawings under the day when they were created. Rule: They must do the entire procedure silently. Anyone who talks will disqualify the entire team.

The first team to complete the task correctly is awarded a prize.

It All Begins With Genesis

LESSON 7

The Days of Creation: A closer look at Days 4-6

Scripture: Genesis 1; Psalm 19:1; 104:1–2; Revelation 21:23–24; Psalm 147:4

Suggested memory verse:

Psalm 19:1 or any verse from Genesis 1

What this lesson is about:

This lesson looks closely at Days 4–6 of Creation, encouraging the student to visualize what the Bible teaches about the events of each Day. The lesson deals with the tough question concerning the light before the creation of the sun, and it also addresses the naturalistic and biblical worldview questions about life and created kinds.

7 C's Connection: Creation

Goals for the lesson: The student should

- know what happened on Days 4–6 of Creation.
- understand these events as biblical truth, not myth.
- be able to describe the two different worldviews and their approach to the origin of life.
- know the difference between an 'evolutionary tree' and a 'creationist orchard.'

Preparation for lesson:

- Work through student's lesson 7.
- 'Props' needed for lesson:

Student drawings for Days 1–3, placed on the time-line bulletin board
Forms to give selected students for Days 4–6 (more information later)
Two sets of eyeglasses, one pair to represent the biblical and one to represent the naturalistic worldview
Word study sign *'bara'* and *'min'* for the word study section of the inductive study bulletin board
Trees and animal cutouts for the baraminology (created kinds) exercise, to go on the bulletin board (computer clip art programs will have many examples to use or you may find pictures in magazines to cut out)

Plan for lesson:

- **Review** the first three Days of Creation. Post the student drawings from last week on the time-line bulletin board. (Don't include drawings with errors, e.g., a shining sun on Day 1. See if the class can spot the errors on these drawings.)

- **Teaching.** Tell students that there seems to be a dilemma. Ask, 'When did God create light and when did God create the sun? Do we have a problem?' Tell them we'll discuss this commonly mentioned problem after they have looked at some Scripture.
- **Class work.** Have the students work through the questions about the purposes of the lights and Psalm 19:1 (the first page of their lesson).
- **Discuss** what they learned from the Scripture. Ask them why God created the universe, according to Genesis 1:14–19 and Psalm 19:1.

  God had a purpose for the lights: separation of day and night, signs, seasons, days and years, and to give light to the earth.

  Psalm 19 helps us to see that the heavens themselves show the glory of God. Ask what we learn about God when we look at the night sky.
- **Teaching.** Discuss the various ways people explain the question of the light created on Day 1 and the sun/moon/stars on Day 4.

  Various explanations:

  1. Shows this is just a myth, a 'story' that has no basis in historical truth.
  2. The sun/moon/stars were actually created on Day 1, but there was a fog or haze and they weren't actually seen until Day 4. (The Hebrew simply doesn't allow this interpretation.)
  3. The Days of Creation are not to be understood chronologically—they serve a literary function, as a 'framework' of Creation not meant to be literal.
  4. God does not need the sun and moon and other light bearers to provide light. He is the source of light.
- **Class work with discussion.** You may wish to work with the students on the second page of their lesson, discussing the content together as you go. (What you do here will depend partly on the time you have available.) Ask them to think about the various explanations as they read Psalm 104:1–2 and then Revelation 21:23 and 22:5.

  You might ask how Psalm 104 answers that question.

  They should be able to tell you that the Lord does not need the sun for light; indeed, there will be no sun in the new heavens and earth. The Lord Himself is the source of light and, no matter how He did it, it did not require the sun.

  Ask, 'What do we learn from Revelation?' (*There will be no need for the sun in the new creation because the glory of God gives the light.)*

  You may also wish to discuss the historical context of Genesis. The book was originally written to slaves just come from Egypt. The Egyptians had a whole pantheon of gods, but the chief god worshipped in Egypt was the sun. It is interesting to speculate that God knew people would some day worship the sun, and He so ordered events in His Creation that people would have no way to think of the sun as the source of all light in the creation.

Ask, 'What is so amazing about **Psalm 147:4**?' (*No man can count all the stars, yet God not only knows how many there are, but He has given names to them.*)

- **Class work. Draw Day 4 of Creation.** (Selected students will draw on the sheets to be posted on the bulletin board; others will draw in their workbooks.)
- **Review.** Using the two large eyeglasses, ask your students if they remember how to define a worldview. Teach the content of 'All about eyeglasses' found on pages 41–42 of their lesson. Define the difference between biblical and naturalistic worldviews.
- **Class work.** Day 5. Assign the questions beginning on the bottom of page 42 of the lesson. What happened on Day 5? What is the repeated phrase? How many times is it repeated? What is God trying to tell us?
- **Discuss.** Discuss (using the eyeglasses) the two worldviews regarding the creation of the different kinds of life.

  First explain about the evolutionary tree (using naturalistic eyeglasses). You could draw a tree on the board and ask if anyone knows the evolutionary progression of this proposed tree (single-celled creatures, sea creatures, amphibians, reptiles, birds, mammals, man). You could ask if this is the same order that they studied for Days 3–5 of Creation.

  Now put on the biblical eyeglasses. Show the students a sign with *bara* and *min*. Discuss the two Hebrew words that mean 'created kind.' Introduce the word 'baraminology' and tell students that this is a new science, one that is classifying living things according to their kinds rather than the current classification system (species/genus/family, etc.) assigned by evolutionary theory.
- **Activity.** Build a creationist orchard on the time-line bulletin board. Place the four trees in the Creation section. (Instructions for this activity are found on the next page.)
- **Class work. Draw Day 5 of Creation.** (Selected students will draw on the sheets to be posted on the bulletin board; others will draw in their workbooks.)
- **Draw Day 6 of Creation.** Tell the students this Day will be studied in detail later. For today, merely draw the pictures.

If you have additional time . . .
Suggestions for augmenting lessons (home school, day school)

Four or five extra sessions would be helpful for this lesson.

There is much to discuss for each Day of Creation. Also, a review of the concept of worldviews, introduced earlier, would be helpful, because this is the first mention of naturalistic and biblical worldviews.

An entire session of the game Zonk would be helpful to review Genesis 1 and all the information about inductive study. Instructions for playing the game Zonk are found at this end of this lesson.

The DVD *Six Short Days, One Big Adventure* presents the Days of Creation in a very entertaining way (35 minute video available at www.AnswersInGenesis.org).

Dr Kurt Wise's lecture 4 *The Days of Creation: A Closer Look* (Precept Ministries) would add to what students have already learned.

Activity: Creationist Orchard

As we look at the world around us, we see an amazing diversity of life. People have sought to classify these different organisms into groups in order to study them better. Those who have an evolutionary understanding of life would suggest that all organisms are one big family. All are part of one big tree. All classification systems we presently see in textbooks reflect this evolutionary presupposition.

Evolutionary tree

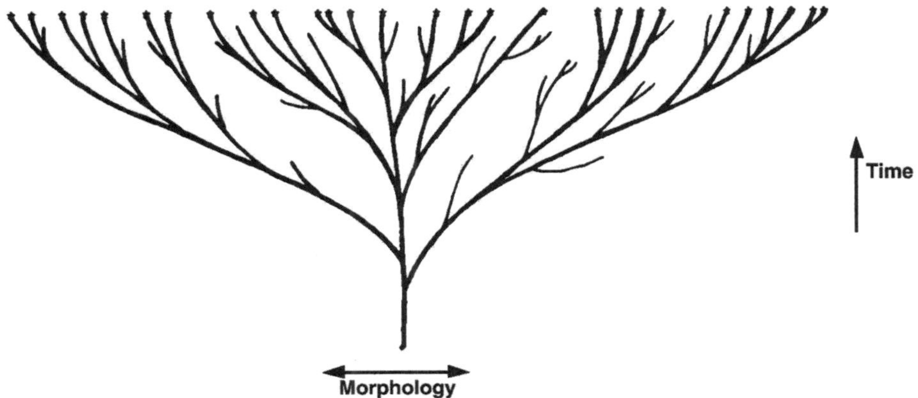

However, the Bible seems to teach that God created a certain number of distinct 'kinds' of organisms. Each of these biblical 'kinds' would be unrelated to other biblical 'kinds.' Instead of an evolutionary 'tree,' we would have an orchard of trees. Within each tree in the orchard would be a variety of related species. Creationists are currently working on a new classification system that would reflect this understanding. The study of created kinds is known as 'baraminology.' The name is taken from two Hebrew words found in Genesis 1: *'bara,'* which means 'create,' and *'min,'* which means 'kind.'

Creationist 'orchard'

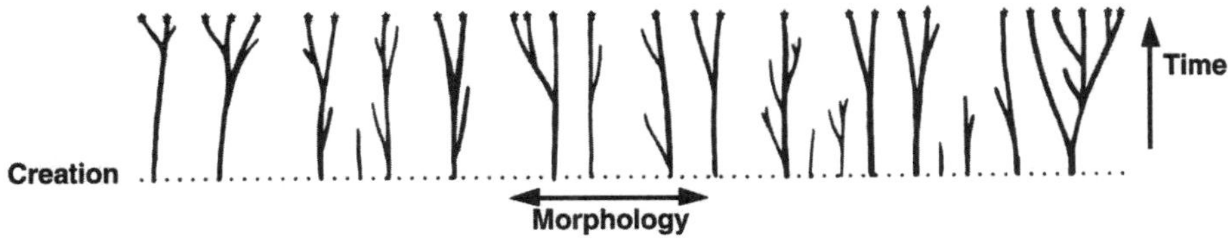

This exercise will help your students understand the concept of baraminology, based upon God's created kinds in Scripture. (Note: Baraminology is a new area of scientific study, and the identification of the precise makeup of baramins is still very much a 'work in progress.' The organisms assigned to a particular baramin will likely change as more research is done. The purpose of this activity is to help students see a pattern in God's creation of living things 'after their kind,' as contrasted with the evolutionary idea of descent from a common ancestor.)

Materials needed:

Pieces of poster board. Draw the trunk of a tree on each. Title them: *Equidae* (horse baramin), *Felidae* (cat baramin), *Canidae* (dog baramin), *Anatidae* (ducks/geese baramin).

Clips of horses, cats, dogs, ducks (computer clip art programs will have many examples to use or you may find pictures in magazines to cut out). Cut out clips and mix them up. You may wish to put them in a zip-lock bag for safekeeping.

Activity: Distribute the mixed cutouts to the students. Allow them to tape or paste the organisms on their appropriate trees. (If you are using the ongoing time-line bulletin board, these trees can be placed under the 'creation' section.)

Activity: Zonk

Zonk is a fantastic review game, enjoyed by teachers and students everywhere (based loosely on the television game show Let's Make a Deal.) To play Zonk you need 52 3x5 cards labeled A–ZZ and another set of 52 cards labeled with a variety of points—100, 200, 300, 400 and 500, along with ten Zonk cards.

To set up your game board, randomly tape the cards on a board, with an alphabet card over each point value or Zonk card.

To play the game, the class is divided into two teams. We alternate which team goes first each week because the team going last has an advantage on continuing to add points. Ask the first team a Bible question, and if it is answered correctly, the child answering the question gets to choose a card on the board, such as CC. Then you lift the card off the board to see what is behind the card, whether points or a zonk.

The child has the choice of continuing to call out cards to accumulate points, as long as he does not get a zonk. If a zonk is picked, the team's turn is over and they lose all the points they have accumulated on their turn. They do not lose any points that are already recorded from a previous turn. A child may stop at any point in choosing cards. Whatever points have accumulated are recorded, as long as the child stops before choosing a zonk. It is now the next team's turn to answer a question. This is continued until all the questions are answered. The team that goes second gets the last question of the game. The team with the most points wins the game, of course.

You will need to come up with your own questions based on what you have covered in class. Some suggested questions are listed at the end of this lesson, but it is a *complete* list of questions about Genesis 1–2 and so it includes questions that have *not* yet been covered in the student workbook.

A	B	C	D	E
F	G	H	I	J
K	L	M	N	O
P	Q	R	S	T
QQ	RR	SS	TT	UU
VV	WW	XX	YY	ZZ

Activity: Jeopardy

Jeopardy is played by having questions labeled into categories of who, what, when/how, where and why, with at least five questions in each category. The easiest question is worth 100 points; the rest are 200 points, 300 points, 400 points or 500 points (the hardest question in each category). The game board is set up with the categories at the top of the board, and the 3x5 cards with point values are taped under each category.

To play the game the class is divided into two teams. The team that goes second always gets the last question. Someone on the first team tells you what category they want to try to answer and what point value they want. For example, the child may say, 'I want "why" for 200 points.' The person in charge of the game will look on the question sheet and choose the 200-point question in the 'why' category. The question is asked, and if it is answered correctly, the team gets the point value they have chosen. After all the questions are asked, the team with the most points wins.

You will need to come up with your own questions based on what you have covered in class. Some suggested questions are listed at the end of this lesson, but it is a *complete* list of questions about Genesis 1–2 and so it includes questions that have *not* yet been covered in the student workbook.

Who?	What?	Why?	Where?	When? How?
100	100	100	100	100
200	200	200	200	200
300	300	300	300	300
400	400	400	400	400
500	500	500	500	500

Questions on Genesis 1–2

100-point questions	What book of the Bible gives the foundation for a biblical worldview? When did God create light? What is the worldview called when the person believes that everything came about by time, chance and natural laws and processes? What is the worldview called that believes God is the Creator of all things and that the world reveals plan, purpose and intelligent design? What warning did God give Adam after he was created and placed in the Garden?
200-point questions	'Said' is repeated ten times in Genesis 1. What kind of word is it? What do you call the beginning of a study, such as the first step in our study (when we looked at all the events of Genesis 1–11 as though we were flying over in a helicopter)? When did God create the fish? When did God create the birds? When did God create man? How would you define a 'presupposition'? What are the are the six 'magic words' of inductive Bible study? When did God create the expanse? *(Day 2)* Choose one: an australopithecine is an *ape* or *man*?
300-point questions	When did God create the stars, sun and moon? *(Day 4)* What is a definition or an example of 'context.' What is the definition of 'worldview'? What did God tell man and animals to eat after they were created? Did God give Adam and Eve any kind of work to do after they were created? What? What does 'catastrophism' mean? Could someone with a biblical worldview believe in evolution? Could someone with a biblical worldview believe in mutations? Could someone with a biblical worldview believe in genetic recombination? Could someone with a biblical worldview believe in natural selection?

400-point questions	**What are the four major events of Genesis 1-11?** **When did God create the land and its vegetation? *(Day 3)*** **What do you learn about the character of God from studying His Creation? (Name two things.)** **What is a 'baramin' (or baraminology)?** **Why are we asking you to mark key words? What good does it do to mark words?** **What is the anthropic principle?** **What is uniformitarianism?**
500-point questions	**What does it mean when we say 'inductive Bible study'?** **If we are doing an inductive study and we reach the part of the study that says 'stop and smell the roses,' what part of the study is that?** **Why are we studying science in Sunday school?** **What is the kind of worldview called that doesn't believe in truth, that believes that 'god' is in everything and that man is his own god? *(pantheistic, transcendental, post-modern)*** **Why were you created? What is your purpose in life? *(to glorify God and enjoy Him forever)***

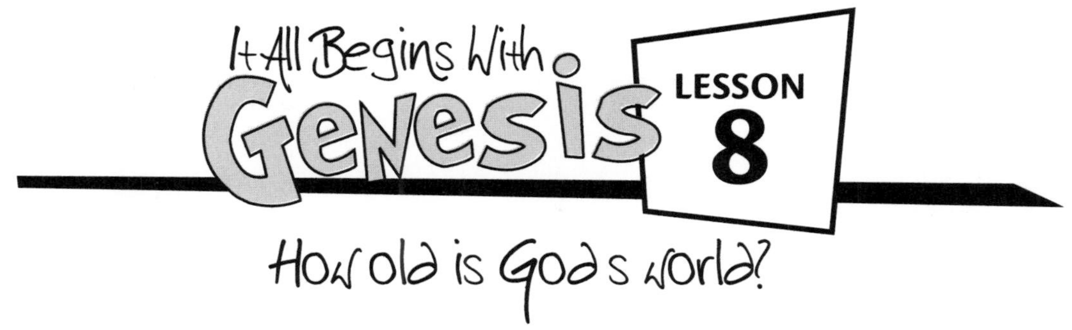

It All Begins With
Genesis
LESSON
8
How old is God's world?

Scripture: Genesis 1; Exodus 20:11; Psalm 33:6; 148:5; 2 Peter 3:8–9

Suggested memory verses:

Exodus 20:11; Psalm 33:6 or 148:5

What this lesson is about:

The age of things is the most hotly debated question in the entire origins issue. It is an area of great controversy even within the church. This lesson doesn't attempt to solve the issue, but rather to lay a beginning foundation on which to help the student make the decision at a later time. All the pieces to the puzzle are not presented in this lesson, but are introduced during the course of the study of Genesis.

In this lesson, the meaning of the word 'day' in Genesis 1 is discussed. The concept of 'context' is introduced at this time. The biblical time line is presented and contrasted with the evolutionary time line. The lesson includes cross-references that can be used to make inferences about age.

7 C's Connection: Creation

Goals for the lesson: The student should

- be able to tell you the different ways 'day' is used in Genesis 1.
- know how to define 'context.'
- be able to describe the two different worldviews and their respective interpretations of the age of things.
- be able to draw a simple time line that shows biblical chronology from Creation until the present, and to recognize the conflict between the biblical chronology and the evolutionary chronology.

Preparation for lesson:

- Work through the student's lesson 8.
- 'Props' needed for lesson:

  Eyeglasses
  'Context is King' sign for inductive Bible study bulletin board (found on the CD, 8-1)
  '*Yom*' word-study sign for inductive Bible study board
  Time line (use colored masking tape with dates, to be added during discussion)
  Optional: A ball of string or yarn marked with paper clips for every million years to show the evolutionary time line. Or you could use a roll of toilet paper, with each square representing one million years.

Plan for lesson:

- **Introduction:** Begin with the two pairs of eyeglasses. When you put on the naturalistic eyeglasses, ask the students what a naturalist would have to believe about the age of things. Then put on the biblical eyeglasses and tell them that there are some Christians who believe the young-age ideas, and others who believe the old-age ideas. Be careful at this point not to press your own particular point of view. Tell them we won't be settling the matter today, but we will begin to look at what the eyewitness account has to say.

- **Introduce the concept of 'context.'** Show a colorful sign you have made that says 'Context is king' (8-1 on the CD that comes with this curriculum). Ask the students if they know what 'context' means.

  Say 'hot dog.' Ask what you mean by that. (They will probably say it is something you eat, or a 'show-off' or a dog on a hot day.) You then ask how they could know which definition you meant when you said the word. They will be able to see that the words and tone you use, in addition to the actual word 'hot dog,' will give the answer. Tell them they have just explained the meaning of context.

  Two more illustrations: the word 'trunk' and the word 'sharp'

  Suggestion. You may wish at this point in the course to take a week away from the assigned lesson to review key points that you want the students to learn. Because of irregular attendance, illness and new visits, some students will have missed important concepts about inductive study, worldviews and Genesis 2. An added week at this time could be helpful.

  If you are able to add a week for review, you could introduce the concept of 'context' in a more detailed fashion. Some suggestions for teaching concept are given at the end of this lesson.

  You also could profitably use extra time to assist in the understanding of the Days of Creation by repeating the 'silent unscramble' game (lesson 6).

  You could review the definition of inductive study and also the definition of worldviews. Help students to see that during this year we have three major objectives: (1) to teach them how to study the Bible inductively; (2) to help them understand worldviews and develop their own biblical worldview; and (3) to study Genesis, the foundation for their worldview.

- **Ask, 'How long is a *yom?*'** Show the class a word study card with the Hebrew word *yom*, meaning 'day.' Ask your class what the different meanings of 'day' could be. List them on the board. (They are on page 48 of their lesson.) Then ask how you would know which meaning is the right meaning? *(Answer: context)*

- **Class work**. Instruct the students to look at the three ways the word is used in Genesis 1 and complete the related exercises in their lesson.

- **Discuss** their answers and then go together to Exodus 20:11 (on page 50) and work it through together. Ask them to give you the context of that verse. Who is speaking? When? What is He doing?

- Ask them to write down their conclusions: Did the writer of Genesis 1 seem to intend 24-hour days or not? Let them know that many people have different ideas about the *yom* issue. Some think the days are long ages; some think they are meant figuratively, not literally; and some say the writer of Genesis 1 just didn't know any better—he was wrong. It isn't fruitful to get into a big discussion of these interpretations at this point—just let them know that serious Christians have different ideas about these things.

- **Put up the biblical time line.** It is helpful to have a time line already posted in the room. Before class, you could add signs for Abraham, Christ and the present. As you go down the time line, have the children tell you where to add your prepared signs for 6 Days (Creation), 1,600 years (Creation to the Flood), 400 years (Flood to Abraham), 2,000 years (Abraham to Christ) and 2,000 years (Christ to present). Have the students fill in their own charts as you go. When you finish the time line, ask them to add up the figures for themselves and record it on their page.

- **Teaching.** Ask if there is a verse in the Bible that tells us the age of the earth and universe. Point to the cross-references given from the genealogies of Genesis 5 and 11 and others to show how the time line is figured out. It is not necessary to take a long time with this.

- **Teaching.** Ask what the naturalistic worldview would say about the age of things. You could then superimpose the biblical time line you made on top of an evolutionary time line. It should be interesting! (You could make the evolutionary time line with clothesline, allowing an inch for every million years, putting clothes pins in the place of the events listed. Or you could use toilet paper, one square for every one million years. Then attempt to put the 6,000-year biblical time line beside it. This exercise makes quite an impression!)

- **Class work and discussion.** Does the Bible give us any other 'clues' about whether God created in a long or short time? Assign the three cross-references given, asking the students to see if they suggest long or short ages for Creation. Discuss their observations.

  Psalm 33:6 discusses the 'breath' of the Lord, suggesting rapidity.

  Psalm 148:5 includes the Hebrew jussive of command, which is used for the commands of kings. It suggests rapid compliance with the command.

  2 Peter 3:8–9 is often used by long-age advocates. It must be seen that the context is the Second Coming of Christ, not the Creation. It does indicate that God Himself is outside of time; He is eternal.

- **The bottom line.** If there is a difference between these two worldviews (and students should definitely see that there is), which will you believe: modern science or the Bible (the eyewitness)? Challenge them during their further study of Genesis to try to determine if indeed the Bible is declaring a young earth. I would not encourage a teacher to push his or her own personal views—merely challenge the students to think and work it out.

If you have additional time . . .
Suggestions for augmenting lessons (home school, day school)

Two extra sessions are recommended, a total of three sessions for this lesson.

The first session would include the supplementary lesson on 'Context is king!' (next three pages). You may wish to use all or part of this supplement. You are free to photocopy these three pages for classroom purposes.

Next, use two sessions to cover the material on the age of things, given in this lesson. This would allow you to cover the cross-references and to do the suggested activities with string etc. You may wish to spend some additional time looking at other non-literal ways that Christians interpret 'day' in Scripture.

Answers in Genesis has several resources available, including *The New Answers Book 1* (chapters 8 and 20) and Ken Ham's talk 'Is Genesis Relevant Today?' (a 30-minute video in the seminar series *Answers ... with Ken Ham*, available on DVD from www.AnswersInGenesis.org).

Context is king!

This lesson supplements the teaching of 'context,' introduced in lesson 8.

1. Let's learn the meaning of the word 'context' through an illustration:

   Suppose I am speaking to you, and I say 'hot dog.' Can you tell what I mean?

   - Perhaps I'm looking at my poor dog George, who is very hot.
   - Perhaps I'm hungry and I want one of those long skinny things on a bun with mustard and chili.
   - Perhaps I'm watching someone play basketball, and he is really showing off.
   - Perhaps I'm excited and want to tell everybody how I feel.

2. How would you know which of these meanings I mean? Write your answer below.

   ____

   The only way you would know what I really mean is by hearing what else I was saying—by hearing the *context,* the other words that surround what I was saying. Was I talking about my dog, or about being hungry, or about basketball or about how excited I was? The other words surrounding the word we looked at tell us the context. You might say the word 'con-text' means 'with text.' You look for what other words surround the text and how all those words are put together. That is the only way to really understand what anyone means. Context is how the Bible is woven together. Knowing the context is the only way to *really* understand the Bible!

3. Let's see if you understand what context is in these examples:

   ✓ Someone tells you that Jesus said you must hate your mother and father. Wow, would Jesus say that? Actually He did say it, in **Luke 14:26** (NAS).

   'If anyone comes to Me, and does not hate his own father and mother and wife and children and brothers and sisters, yes, and even his own life, he cannot be My disciple.'

   When you read the *context* of the verse, you learn he is saying that He must be first in our lives, and compared to Him, we should 'hate' everything and everyone else. He doesn't mean what we normally think when we hear the word 'hate.' The context, or the words surrounding the word 'hate,' teaches us the true meaning.

   ✓ In **Psalm 57:1,** it says we hide in the shelter of God's wings. Look at that verse below.

   'Be gracious to me, O God, be gracious to me, for my soul takes refuge in You; and in the shadow of Your wings I will take refuge, until destruction passes by' (NAS).

   Hmmm . . . could that mean God looks something like a chicken? Of course not! Psalm 57 uses a lot of figurative, or picture, language to tell us how God cares for us. Context tells us the meaning.

✓ In another passage we are told to put on armor. Does that mean that Christians are to go around like the medieval knights wearing armor?

Ephesians 6:11–14 (NAS) 'Put on the full armor of God, that you may be able to stand firm against the schemes of the devil. For our struggle is not against flesh and blood, but against the rulers, against the powers, against the world forces of this darkness, against the spiritual forces of wickedness in the heavenly places. Therefore, take up the full armor of God, that you may be able to resist in the evil day, and having done everything, to stand firm. Stand firm therefore, having girded your loins with truth, and having put on the breastplate of righteousness.'

Look at the context of Ephesians 6 and write below what is meant by wearing armor.

____

____

____

4. Are you beginning to get the idea of context? See what you think about the meaning of the sample verses below. Read each verse from Scripture and mark the correct answer from the choices you are given.

✓ **1 Kings 18:27** (NAS) . . . either he is occupied or gone aside, or is on a journey, or perhaps he is asleep and needs to be awakened.'

	Your pastor doesn't answer when you knock on his office door.
	Elijah is mocking the prophets of Baal because their god is not able to do anything.

(How could you *really* know the correct answer, unless you went to the Bible and saw the context of the verse?)

✓ **1 Corinthians 15:51** (NAS) . . . we will not all sleep, but we will all be changed.'

	God is telling us what is going to happen if we are alive when Christ returns.
	This is a sign on a nursery door.

✓ **1 Chronicles 11:9** (KJV) 'So David waxed greater and greater: for the Lord of hosts was with him.'

	David was waxing the floor of the castle.
	God blessed David, and he became greater and greater.

✓ **Isaiah 55:2** (KJV) . . . eat ye that which is good, and let your soul delight itself in fatness.'

	The Bible tells us to eat a lot and get fat.
	Many blessings will come to those who know and seek the Lord.

Game: context of silly sounds

This activity is another way to learn context.

Materials needed: 3x5 cards and markers or pens

Preparation: Write out each of the following sentences on a 3x5 card. (Don't write what the silly word stands for.)

- Maybe it will *geebo* today. The weatherman did predict storms. (geebo = rain)
- She's such a wonderful *whappet*. We've known each other since first grade, and we've hardly ever had a fight. (whappet = friend)
- He says he has to go to *spersh* practice today. He hopes that coach will show them the new helmets. (spersh = football)
- The s'mores are her favorite part of *gleeking*, because sometimes bugs get in the tents and sleeping bags. (gleeking = camping)
- He sometimes frightens little children. All they see is a big *baney* with a wagging tail that wants to lick their face. (baney = dog)
- Go get the sleds! It's beginning to *pleep!* (pleep = snow)
- Everyone hide, and when he walks in the room, yell, 'Happy *zadoot!*' Then I'll bring out the cake. (zadoot = birthday)
- We went to see a *kobber* last night. I didn't like it very much, but the popcorn was good. (kobber = movie)
- It was so hot that she had to pull her *nobba* off of her neck and put it in a ponytail. (nobba = hair)

Procedure:

1. Explain to the class that context means 'from text.' It means that you can tell what a word or phrase means by looking at the sentences that are around it.
2. Tell the children that you are going to read them a sentence or two. One word will be a silly word that stands for a real word. They have to listen to the context to figure out what the silly word stands for.

If you want, you can also divide the class into two teams and then read the cards to them. The first team that guesses the correct meaning of the silly word gets a point.

It All Begins With Genesis

LESSON 9

God's special creation: man!

Scripture: Genesis 1 and 2

Suggested memory verse:

Genesis 2:7

What this lesson is about:

Understanding that man as a special creation of God, made in God's image, is key to developing a sound Biblical worldview. This lesson begins a three-week study of Genesis 2. This lesson includes an overview of Genesis 2 and practice in inductive study skills, and it teaches the new skill of making a list based on a key word.

7 C's Connection: Creation

Goals for the lesson: The student should

- be able to define a 'key word' and understand that lists can be made from these words.
- have a basic understanding of the events of Genesis 2.
- see more clearly the hand of a loving Creator as He formed man and provided for him.

Preparation for lesson:

- Work through the student's lesson 9.
- 'Props' needed for this lesson:

  Review sheets on the inductive study bulletin board: four steps of inductive study

  Transparencies for Genesis 1 and 2, overhead projector

Plan for lesson:

- **Introduction.** Review the four steps of inductive study. See if they remember (1) the helicopter—overview; (2) hiking—chapter study; (3) stop and smell the roses—word study; (4) satellite—cross-references. Point out how they have completed each of the steps already. Now it is time to go back to the chapter study, this time using Genesis 2. (You can use visuals for this by taking the signs off the bulletin board or preparing transparencies that illustrate the steps.)
- **Teaching.** Instruct students to take out their observation sheets for Genesis 1–2 and turn to lesson 9 in their notebook. As a group, work through the questions on the first page of the lesson. Help them to see the way Genesis is organized through the repeated phrase 'This is the account of ...'.

- **Class work.** Assign three key words for them to mark in Genesis 2: God, man, woman. You might wish to draw on the board suggested ways to mark these words. Use a purple crown for God, blue stick figure for man, pink stick figure for woman. Be sure they understand the need to mark the pronouns and synonyms as well.
- **Discuss.** Explain how marking key words will help them to make lists of what they learn. The student book has a chart to help students walk through a list on God's dealings with man.
- **Class work.** Complete the chart given in the student lesson. (If time is short and your class is large, you may wish to assign parts of the chart to different students.)
- **Discussion.** List on the board what was learned about God/man/woman from making the chart.

  You could ask questions such as these:

  Do you think God really cared a lot about man? What makes you think so?
  How does God's creation of man differ from His creation of animals? (He really got his hands dirty, didn't He?) What kinds of things did God provide for man?

  You will have more to discuss than time available, at this point. In the little time you have, try to encourage the students to react to what they see—to make some interpretations of their observations. Most of all you want them to see the character of God as He lovingly creates man and provides for all his needs.

Suggested illustrations and activities:

You most likely won't have time in a regularly scheduled class to complete all that is included in this lesson. If time does permit, and if students can work at home with their materials, it would be very helpful for them to complete all the questions in the margin of their observation sheet. They then could choose the theme and draw a picture of Genesis 2.

If you have additional time . . .
Suggestions for augmenting lessons (home school, day school)

At least two extra sessions would be helpful with this lesson. Take one entire session to allow the students to go through the observations for Genesis 2, answering the questions in the margin.

Since this week introduces how to make lists from key words ('God' in this lesson), it would also be helpful to make some lists of other key words or phrases. Constant review and reinforcement of the inductive study concepts and the worldview concepts are needed.

It All Begins With Genesis

LESSON 10

How special are you?

Scripture: Genesis 2; Job 33:4; Psalm 100:3; 119:73; Isaiah 43:7; 64:8; Psalm 8:3–9; John 3:16

Suggested memory verse:

Choose from any of the above passages.

What this lesson is about:

The understanding that man is a special creation of God, made in God's image, is key to developing a sound biblical worldview. This lesson is the second in a three-week study of Genesis 2. This lesson includes cross-references that focus on God's view of man. There is much opportunity for application of the principles here to the worldviews we see around us. This lesson reinforces two inductive study principles—cross-references and the Five W's and H.

7 C's Connection: Creation, Christ, Cross

Goals for the lesson: The student should

- understand the difference between a naturalistic and a biblical worldview concerning the origin of mankind.
- clearly see how special he is in God's eyes, and be able to say why.
- define 'cross-reference.'
- grow in his ability to interrogate the text with who, what, where, when, why and how questions.

Preparation for lesson:

- Work through the student's lesson 10.
- 'Props' needed for lesson: play dough or clay for 'potter and clay' illustration; a crown for 'child of the king' illustration; worldview eyeglasses

Plan for lesson:

- **Introduction.** For this illustration you will need a big lump of clay, preferably a very big lump. When the students arrive in the room, they should observe you busily creating something that looks rather strange—you can be very imaginative! They will ask you what you are doing when they arrive, but just look mysterious and keep working intently on your creation. Wait until late in the lesson to explain your purpose.
- **Review.** Ask the students if they can remember what Genesis 2 talked about the most. Discuss what was 'special' about the way God created man. (God 'got His hands dirty.')

- **Teach.** Today's class will help us see what the whole Bible has to say about how God cares about man. We will be looking at cross-references (You can ask them if they know what step of inductive study we are doing.)

  You might illustrate the two worldviews concerning mankind at this point. Ask two students to offer to stand in front of the class. One student represents the naturalistic worldview. He can be asked to look sad because he believes he just happened by chance, has no purpose, etc. The other student is given a crown to wear—he is a child of the king. Do not go into any more detail at this time, but tell the students that we will be looking at just what a difference this really makes.

  Begin once again with the two pairs of eyeglasses. See if the students can tell you what the naturalistic and biblical worldviews would say about mankind.

- **Class work.** Assign the cross-references in the lesson. Remind students about the Five W's and H kinds of questions. (You could ask how we knew what kind of questions to ask. *Answer: the text answered a particular question—we only found what question was answered.*) You may wish to give the students the opportunity to do the work quietly and independently, or you can go through each passage and ask someone to read the verse and other students to answer.

- **Discuss.** As you go through the cross-references (sections 1–10), make a summary list on the board. You could title the list 'God's plan for me.' Teach the students to identify the reference and to be precise in their answers, using words from the text and not paraphrases. Your list would look something like this:

  God's plan for me

  God made me; the breath of the Almighty gave me life (Job 33:4).

  God made us. We are His people, the sheep of His pasture (Psalm 100:3).

  He made me and formed me. I need to ask for understanding to learn His commands (Psalm 119:73).

  God formed and made me, called me by His name, made us sons and daughters, made me for His glory (Isaiah 43:6–7).

  God is our Father, the Potter; we are the clay, the work of His hand (Isaiah 64:8).

  God is mindful of me and cares for me. God made me a little lower than heavenly beings and crowned me with glory and honor. God made me ruler and put everything under my feet: flocks, herds, beasts of the field, birds of the air, fish of the sea (Psalm 8:3–9).

  God so loved me that He gave His own Son. He gives eternal life to all who believe in Him (John 3:16).

- Return now to your clay 'masterpiece.' Tell students that this is a very special creation that *you* made. It is your creation, and the work of your hands. Because you are the creator of this masterpiece, the following things are true:

    You own the creation.

    You can give the creation a name, because you made it.

    You know the purpose for which you created it.

    You are the one who can change it or even destroy it, because you made it and formed it.

    You can place the price on the creation. You determine its value.

    You know how this creation needs to be handled for its best good—you make the rules for this creation.

  Ask students what they learn about God and about themselves from this illustration. *(They are very special creations of God. They are* ***His*** *creation, and He places the value on this creation.)* Ask how great a value He placed on your students. *(He died for them. He named them, because He made them. He is the one who knows for what purpose they were created. He owns them; He sets the rules. Because He created them, He knows what is best for His created beings. He can also change and mold us, and He can judge us.)*

Final discussion. Return now to your stand-up illustration of the two worldviews: the child of chance and the child of the king. Ask the students to compare the results of the two worldviews (pages 62–63 in their lesson). What would be the purpose of life? How would you decide what is right and wrong and how to live?

If you have additional time . . .
Suggestions for augmenting lessons (home school, day school)

This lesson is shorter and can probably be adequately covered in one session.

It All Begins With Genesis

LESSON 11

Life before sin came into the world

Scripture: Genesis 1–2, Isaiah 11:6–9, Revelation 21–22 (selected passages)

Suggested memory verse:

Choose any verses from Genesis 2.

What this lesson is about:

This lesson is the last in the three-lesson study of Genesis 2. This lesson's focus is the perfect world that God created. In order to understand future lessons on the Fall, sin and death, it is important for the student to see God's ideal for the world. Genesis 1–2 tells us. The prophetic passages in Isaiah and Revelation also give us God's perspective on what He considers good.

7 C's Connection: Creation, Consummation

Goals for the lesson: The student should

- understand what life in the Garden was like before sin came into the world. He should see God's original design in relationships, in food, in work, in climate.
- see what God's ideal world is like as expressed in prophetic passages of Isaiah and Revelation. He should see some parallels with God's original creation.
- eventually see (after studying the Fall) just how serious the biblical Fall really was.

Preparation for lesson:

- Work through the student's lesson 11.
- Props: Prepare a sign for the Genesis bulletin board 'God looked on all He created and behold, it was very good.' You will place the students' drawings of 'Life before sin came into the world' under the sign.

Plan for lesson:

- **Introduction.** Ask the students if they ever thought about what a 'perfect' world would be like. Give them some time to imagine that kind of world. Ask them, 'What kind of world did God originally create?' (Genesis 1:31). 'So, would you say today's world is very good?' (Consider, for example, stinging insects, animals eating each other, earthquakes and other natural disasters.) 'What happened?'
- **Class work.** Instruct the students to go to lesson 11 in their books and take out their observation sheets for Genesis 1–2 and their colored pencils. Ask students to mark 'garden' on their observation sheet for Genesis 2, and make a list of what they learned (question 2 on page 65 of their student workbook).

- **Discuss** what they learned from their work time. Write a list on the board as they give their answers. (They should be learning how to make lists: include the verse number and the answer, with words from the text.) The list should look something like this:
  - 8 planted by the LORD God; east in Eden; God placed man there
  - 9 LORD God caused trees to grow; pleasing to sight and good for food; Tree of Life in midst of Garden; Tree of Knowledge of Good and Evil
  - 10 Water flowed out of Eden to water the Garden and divided into four rivers
  - 15 God put man into Garden to cultivate and keep it
  - 16 God told man he could eat from any tree but not of the Tree of Knowledge of Good and Evil, or he would die
- **Class work.** Instruct students to draw what they have learned so far on page 71 of their worksheet: 'Life before sin came into the world.'
- **Class work.** There remain two different groupings of questions. The first includes questions about Genesis 1–3 concerning life in the Garden (sections 3–10). The second group of questions relates to cross-references in Isaiah and Revelation (sections 11–12). This is a large assignment. You may prefer to split the class and have each group work on a different assignment. Or you may wish to assign only the Genesis references as class work and discuss the Isaiah and Revelation passages as a group.
- **Discuss** the insights learned from the cross-references.

If you have additional time . . .
Suggestions for augmenting lessons (home school, day school)

Suggested: two extra sessions associated with this lesson

The cross-references are extensive and more time would allow the students to complete them in a thoughtful manner. The final session could include a Zonk game for review because the course study of Genesis pauses after this lesson and the worldview section begins.

Class work. Encourage the students to add to the drawings begun earlier in the lesson, because they now have additional information to include. Post these drawings on the time-line bulletin board under 'Life before sin.' If you are unable to do the complete time line, you could use a large piece of poster board and post on it the drawings done by the students.

It All Begins With Genesis

LESSON 12

Recognizing different worldviews in Scripture (part 1)

Scripture: John 2:1–10

Suggested memory verse:

John 17:17

What this lesson is about:

This lesson continues to build upon the concept of worldviews introduced at the very first lesson. Children are going to be confronted by many ideas that are anti-biblical. The biblical worldview is no longer the dominant view seen in the media, in politics or in education. Christian young people need to be able to discern what worldview is operating behind what is presented. In this lesson and the lessons to come, we will seek to help students learn to recognize the presuppositions that drive worldviews. They need to recognize that one's view of God determines one's view of the world. We will examine the different worldviews found in Scripture, in the society and in the science classroom.

7 C's Connection: Creation, Corruption

Goals for the lesson: The student should

- know the meaning of the word 'presupposition' and how it affects our worldview.
- know the presuppositions that someone with a naturalistic worldview holds.
- see how naturalistic presuppositions are illustrated in the Cana 'water-to-wine' event of John 2.
- understand that all teaching, however 'reasonable,' must be evaluated in the light of biblical truth.

Preparation for lesson:

- Work through the student's lesson 12.
- 'Props' needed for lesson:

  Worldview eyeglasses
  Sign with 'A presupposition is ...'
  Props for skit: you might include a scarf for Mary, a robe for Jesus, an apron for the headwaiter, a cup of 'wine' and something to represent the 30-gallon stone pots.

12 Recognizing different worldviews in Scripture (part 1)

Plan for lesson:

- **Review and introduce the next series of lessons (lessons 12–19).** We are beginning a series of lessons that seek to enlarge and clarify the concept of worldviews. There will be a temporary delay of lessons on Genesis and a look at scientific and cultural issues. It would be helpful to point out this shift in focus to the students.

  If you have constructed bulletin boards for inductive study, worldview and the Genesis time line, you can easily review with the students the three major goals for the class this year. See if they can tell you.

  1. How to study the Bible inductively

  2. How to understand worldviews and build a biblical worldview

  3. The Book of Genesis, the foundation of the Word of God

  You can then go on to explain that the next eight lessons will focus on goal 2.

- **Teach** the meaning of the word 'presupposition.' Show students a large sign (or overhead transparency) with the word 'presupposition' on it. Tell them this is an important '50-cent word' they will learn today. See if they can give a definition from what 'pre-' and 'suppose' mean. Then go into some examples, lots of examples. Some examples are given in the lesson (sections 3–5), and you can probably think of others that are timely and appropriate to your particular group.

- **Class work.** Take the group through the review of worldview definitions and definitions of the naturalistic and biblical worldviews in section 6 (pages 75 and 76) of the lesson. The 'fill in the blank' questions on page 76 should be answered as follows:

  How did the world _come to be or get here_?
  Is there a _God_?
  If there is a _God_, what is He _like_?
  How did I _get here_?
  Who am I?
  What is my _purpose_ in life?
  Where did evil _come from_?
  How then should _I live_?

- **Role-play** the wedding at Cana found in **John 2:1–10.** The script is included in the student lesson. You will need the following players: narrator, Jesus, Mary, master of banquet, bridegroom and servants.

- **Class work and discussion.** Answer the questions on pages 78–80.

  Encourage students to reason how the master of the banquet might have seen the truth if he were looking for it. (Some people knew about what had happened: the servants, Mary and, of course, Jesus. Holding the best wine until late in the feast was totally against tradition. The containers were huge pots used for the Jewish purification ritual—wine would not have been kept in them. It was perfect wine, better than anything he had ever tasted. That could have made him curious and prompted him to seek where the wine had actually originated.)

  Ask why people have trouble believing miracles can happen. *(They have naturalistic presuppositions.)* Ask the students to tell you some of the other events reported in Scripture that contemporary people would not have believed because there was not a naturalistic explanation for it. *(The Resurrection, etc.)*

  See if the students can tell you why it is important for them to recognize the naturalistic presuppositions behind things they are taught. Ask them what they should do when they hear something taught that goes against what they know the Bible teaches.

  The final question asks the students to write down something important they learned from the lesson. If time permits, this could be a good discussion. Some of their responses might include the following:

  The meaning of a 'presupposition.'
  How presuppositions can influence your worldview.
  A person's reasoning can be reasonable, but still wrong.
  I need to go to the eyewitness (the Word of God).
  I need to question and think about things and expect God to work.
  When God does something, it can look like it took a very long time if we are wearing naturalistic eyeglasses.

If you have additional time . . .
Suggestions for augmenting lessons (home school, day school)

This lesson can be accomplished in one session. The students will need much reinforcement of the word 'presupposition,' and additional illustrations would be helpful. Answers in Genesis has several helpful resources, including *Evolution Exposed: Biology* (see chapter 1; the book is available from www.AnswersInGenesis.org).

LESSON 13

Recognizing different worldviews in Scripture (Part 2)

(Note: This lesson may be difficult for the younger students. If you do not have adequate time for all the lessons presented in this curriculum, you should probably omit this lesson.

Another way you could include the material—which gives good practice in inductive skills—is to send the lesson home with the students. Ask them to complete the lesson on their own, and provide some form of reward for those who make the effort to study for themselves.)

Scripture: Romans 1:18–32

Suggested memory verse:

Romans 1:20–23 (or a portion of it)

What this lesson is about:

This lesson continues to build upon the concept of worldviews introduced in the very first lesson. This passage in Romans not only describes the worldview of someone who denies God, but it shows the consequences of this behavior. While this is a somber and difficult passage, it is a vital one.

This lesson also continues to offer students experience in inductively studying biblical text, teaching them to ask who, what, where, when, why and how questions and to understand Scripture more clearly from their answers.

7 C's Connection: Corruption

Goals for the lesson: The student should

- understand from Romans 1 what can be learned about God from His creation (general revelation).
- understand why God is angry.
- understand what men are doing and why they have no excuse.
- understand what happens when God 'gives them over.'
- be able to discuss this process as seen in our world today.

Plan for lesson:

- It is always helpful to review, especially when last week's lesson was dealing with presuppositions and examples from Scripture. See if students remember what a presupposition is. See if they can tell you what they learned from looking at the headwaiter at the wedding.

- **Class work.** Give students most of the remainder of the time to work through Romans 1:18–32 on their own.
- **Suggestion**. Because this curriculum is a full one, you may need to cut some lessons if you do not have enough weeks to cover the material. This lesson could be "optional." Although the Romans 1 passage is an important creation passage, this lesson tends to be difficult for younger students. You may wish to omit this lesson entirely or use it for a take-home lesson, where students can practice their inductive study skills and discuss the material with their parents.

If you have additional time . . .
Suggestions for augmenting lessons (home school, day school)

Additional sessions are not required for this lesson. This lesson will serve as a good evaluation of how well the students are picking up the concepts of inductive study.

After they have completed the questions on their own, go through the questions with them. Encourage practical application to their lives.

It All Begins With Genesis

LESSON 14

Recognizing different worldviews in our culture

Suggested memory verse: Romans 2:20–23 (or a portion of it)

What this lesson is about:

This lesson continues to build upon the concept of worldviews. It seeks to help students recognize the behavior that follows certain belief systems. The suggested 'skit' is an interesting way to present the information.

7 C's Connection: Creation

Goals for the lesson: The student should

- be able to define the three major worldviews in our culture today. The pantheistic worldview (transcendental, post-modern) is introduced for the first time in this lesson.
- be able to identify how a person's presuppositions about God (his 'God' view) drive his understanding of his world and his behavior in it.
- consider how the biblical worldview is more compelling and explains reality better than the alternate worldviews.

Preparation for lesson:

- Work through student's lesson 14.
- Invite three adults to play the parts of the naturalist, pantheist and theist. Give them copies of the chart at the end of this lesson. Encourage them to improvise and dress for the part if possible (e.g. the theist could hold a Bible, the naturalist could wear a white lab coat, and the transcendentalist could wear flowers or other 'hippie' garb.)
- Prepare three signs for the guests to hold: Professor Green, naturalist; Barry Bible, theist; Post-modern Madge, pantheist (available on the CD that comes with this curriculum).

Plan for lesson:

- Review presuppositions. Ask if someone can give you the definition of the word. Ask how a presupposition can affect the way a person acts or lives. Give lots of illustrations. A few suggestions follow. You can probably think of some personal ones that will be familiar to your class.

  Presupposition: Mom and Dad like your sister or brother better than you.

  Result: You are jealous of your sister; you may mistreat her; you will constantly be interpreting things your parents do in the light of that presupposition.

Presupposition: Someone told you when you were a child that you were 'chubby.' You begin to think you are fat, even if you are not.

Result: You see 'fat' whenever you look in a mirror. You are self-conscious and buy 'fat' clothes. You may even develop an eating disorder, such as anorexia or bulimia.

Presupposition: You are convinced that God loves you and has the best plan for you and your life. You trust Him.

Result: When illness or other difficult times come, you are able to stand firm and stay at peace, knowing the joy of the Lord.

- There are several ways you can use the skit found in the lesson. If you have a group setting, the best way is probably to ask three adults to role-play the three people described. Begin by introducing each person and spending some time explaining the presuppositions each holds. Have them sit in front of the class. It would be helpful to give them each a sign to hold that identifies them by name and worldview.
- You could then pose the interview questions to each person in turn. Since the script is included in the student lesson, you could ask them as you go what they think is the correct response to each question. (Give them a copy of the answers, provided on pages T-73 to T-74.) The lesson is set up in such a way that each student could do his own work quietly and then come back and discuss it.
- Encourage discussion. Ask students which view they believe is true. Ask how each person's view of God affects his view of the world. Which person has the best explanation for the world we see?

If you have additional time . . .
Suggestions for augmenting lessons (home school, day school)

No additional sessions are required for this lesson. However, if you have a mature group of students, they would benefit from watching Dr Kurt Wise's lecture 6 from the Precept *Genesis 1* series, on worldviews.

It might be helpful to point out that many people have a mixture of these worldviews. For example, many who consider themselves Christian have naturalistic presuppositions and deny miracles and accept evolution. Others within the church merge pantheistic ideas, such as reincarnation, in their way of thinking.

	Professor Green	Post-modern Madge	Barry Bible
How does one find his way to God?	There is no God. Man invented Him.	There are many ways to god. All is god.	Jesus is the way. No man comes to the Father but by Him.
When you go outside on a beautiful fall day, what do you see?	I see Mother Nature! Look at all the wonders of evolution. It is amazing what has developed over all these billions of years.	I see the Force! God everywhere! He is in the rocks, the trees and the birds. We are all divine, and we are one with nature.	I see the awesome creation of an awesome God. The whole creation shouts out His glory! I also see a fallen world. There are sad things here because man fell into sin.
How did life happen?	It just happened! It came from primordial ooze and evolved upward over billions of years.	We call it cosmic evolution. There is this mysterious force that has been around from eternity, recycling its power, going from disharmony to harmony.	In the beginning God created the heavens and the earth.
How can you know something is true?	We know from human reason, experience, modern science and rational thought.	There is no truth. What is true for you might not be true for me. As long as it is meaningful to *you*, that is what really matters.	Jesus is the Truth. God has revealed truth to us in the Scriptures and through His Holy Spirit.
Just who is man?	He is a highly evolved animal.	He is a spiritual being who is a god. He is fundamentally perfect.	He is a creature made in the image of God and precious to God. He is also a sinner in need of God's salvation.

	Professor Green	Post-modern Madge	Barry Bible
What do you believe is responsible for all the crime we see today?	It is the fault of society. There is so much ignorance and superstition. More education and more money should solve the problems.	Poor choices. You decide the value of life based on your culture. Our society stifles our knowledge of the god within. Our culture ignores human potential.	Crime is the result of sinners in rebellion against a holy God.
How do you understand the problem of racism?	It is an evolutionary thing. Some groups have climbed higher in the evolutionary scale than others, while others are basically inferior. We need education and a stronger government to stop the problems that arise.	The group identity is all that is important. It is how we identify with our culture. It is important to connect with your group.	We are all descended from Noah and his sons—we are one family. There is no basis for racial discrimination. All Christians are one in Christ Jesus.
What is your view of the Bible?	It is not true. Primitive men wrote it. It is full of myths and stories. The only things that we can accept are what man today can reason are true. Science, not an ancient book, must show us the way.	It is basically irrational. Religion is a choice. There are many ways to god. If the Bible is good for some, that is fine.	It is the revealed, true Word of God.
How can humans solve their problems today?	By scientific technology and advancement. By spending more money.	By a transformation of consciousness. Just by love.	By salvation—by faith in the finished work of Christ.

It All Begins With Genesis

LESSON 15

Recognizing different worldviews in science (part 1)

Scripture: Genesis 1:16; Nehemiah 9:6; Isaiah 40:22; Job 9:9; Isaiah 40:26; Jeremiah 32:17; Hebrews 11:3

Suggested memory verse:

Jeremiah 32:17

What this lesson is about:

Lessons 15–19 will contrast the naturalistic and biblical worldviews in the scientific areas of the origin of the universe, rocks and fossils, life, groups of life, and mankind. Today's lesson focuses on the views of the origin of the universe. The challenging questions to be asked of each view: Is it reasonable? Is it true? Is it compelling? What does the eyewitness say?

7 C's Connection: Creation

Goals for the lesson: The student should

- be able to see the presuppositions behind the definitions of 'science' given in the lesson.
- be able to define the 'big bang' naturalistic approach to the origin of the universe as well as the 'anthropic principle,' which takes into account the biblical view.
- increase in his critical ability to think and discern the presuppositions about God that influence various interpretations of origins.
- know what the eyewitness, Scripture, has to say about the origin of the universe.

Preparation for lesson:

- Work through student's lesson 15.
- Props for lesson:

  Chocolate chip cookies

  Three illustrations/overheads (all on the CD that comes with this curriculum): 'The heavens declare the glory of God' (15-1); 'Origin of the universe: naturalism would say' (15-2); 'The anthropic principle' (15-3)

  Matching game on the anthropic principle (instructions and cutouts at the end of this lesson)

- Prepare an illustration on the 'Origin of the universe: which is compelling,' to be added to the worldview bulletin board, contrasting the two worldviews (15-4 on the curriculum CD).

Plan for lesson:

- **Introduction.** Present the class with a plate of chocolate chip cookies. Ask if they remember the 'delicious cake' activity that you used on the first class this year. Tell them these cookies are 'data.' Ask them to come up with various ideas about the origin of these cookies. *(Your teacher baked them; she bought them at the store; someone else baked them and gave them to her; they formed naturalistically over many years after chocolate chips, eggs, flour and butter sat on a surface, etc.)* Ask them what presuppositions people might have that would affect their interpretation of the origin of this data. *(Someone knows your teacher hates to cook and never cooks, someone has eaten her chocolate chip cookies before, someone hates chocolate, etc.)*

  Principles you want them to learn from this type of exercise:

  1. Everyone looks at the same data. (In other words, everyone sees the same chocolate chips, consistency of the cookies, the amount of various ingredients, taste; etc.)
  2. Often different interpretations of the same data are given. (The cookies taste good, they taste bad, they were homemade, they were bought at a bakery, etc.)
  3. Often, all or many of the interpretations seem reasonable.
  4. Being reasonable doesn't necessary make an interpretation true.
  5. Presuppositions strongly influence people's interpretation.
  6. The eyewitness report is extremely valuable when sorting out truth. Ask if there is an eyewitness to the making of the cookies.

- **Discuss definitions of science.** Refer students to the two definitions of science found on the first page of their lesson for today. Teach them the meaning of the word 'science' (Latin word for 'knowledge'). Read the two definitions and see if students can tell the worldview behind each. *(The first is the naturalistic; the second, the biblical.)* Explain to them that you desire to help them learn to spot the worldview behind the things they are taught in school, at museums, etc., as they search for truth.

- **Teach.** Put up a transparency (or poster) with an image of the universe (15-1 on the curriculum CD). Tell students that this is the 'data' we are looking at today. Instruct students to pretend they have a naturalistic worldview and do not believe there is a God. Ask them to use their imaginations and write down an explanation for how all these stars, galaxies, etc., came to be. You can then allow some of the students to read their explanations. (Don't spend a lot of time on this.)

- **Teach.** Use the illustration that presents the naturalistic worldview of 'big bang' cosmology (15-2). You might use this time to discuss the 'big bang' and the evidence for it *(expanding universe, background radiation).* Ask if this view sounds reasonable? *(Some will say yes; others no. Point out that this is the most popular cosmogony—story of the origin of the universe—around today. Some may see the problems inherent in producing order from an explosion.)* Your point here is not a detailed explanation or critique of the 'big bang,' but simply a presentation of the naturalistic explanation of the origin of the universe.
- Ask, 'Is there another way of looking at this data?'
- Use the illustration of the anthropic principle (15-3). Ask if anyone knows what 'anthropic' means. *(It comes from the Greek word for 'man.')* Have the students write the definition in the designated spot in the lesson.
- **Activity.** The 'silent matching game on the anthropic principle' (instructions on page T-79). After the students have found their 'partner' who has the matching fact about the universe, ask them to stand when their number is called and read to the class. You can emphasize some of the facts after they are read. When they finish the oral presentations, direct the students to the facts that are written in their lesson. See if they can remember the answers from the oral presentation, and have them write the facts down.
- **Teach.** Use the illustration that presents the two views (15-4). Ask, 'Are they both reasonable? Which is more compelling to you and why? Where do we find the eyewitness account here?'
- **Class work.** Assign the Scriptures given in the lesson. You can read and discuss them as a group, or you can assign the work and then discuss the answers together.

  Points of emphasis:

  Genesis 1:16. God made the sun, moon, stars.

  Nehemiah 9:6. Our response to Him should be worship/awe.

  Isaiah 40:22. Bring out that the Bible does not teach a flat earth. There are several places where the earth is referred to as a circle or sphere. Also, the Bible in several places refers to a 'stretched out' heaven. This would suggest an expanding universe. Just because there is an expanding universe does not mean the naturalistic explanation for its origin is true.

  Job 9:9. Note the Bible's knowledge of the constellations. God's creative design is in view here.

  Isaiah 40:26. Nobody even knows how many stars there are in the universe, yet our powerful God calls each by name.

  Jeremiah 32:17. We know that nothing is too hard for our Sovereign Creator God. Ask students what that truth means in their life.

Hebrews 11:3. The universe was formed at God's command. God made the things we see out of things not visible. We understand these things by faith.

(You want to work on having the students be very precise in what they answer—let them respond with the words of Scripture, not with paraphrases that merely sound spiritual but are not addressing the exact words in the passage.)

If you have additional time ...
Suggestions for augmenting lessons (home school, day school)

One to three extra sessions would be helpful with this lesson.

One session could focus on presuppositions behind the definition of science, a review of naturalistic/theistic worldviews, and the naturalistic 'big bang.'

There are several excellent resources that explain the big bang from a biblical perspective. *The New Answers Book 2* (chapter 10), *Taking Back Astronomy* by Dr. Jason Lisle, and the 'Big Bang' DVD from the *Answers Academy* curriculum. *Answers* magazine volume 3.1 (and the AiG website) has articles dedicated to astronomy topics (available from www.AnswersInGenesis.org).

Silent matching game on the anthropic principle

'Anthropic principle' comes from the Greek word for man, *'anthropos.'* The anthropic principle states that the universe is especially suited for the well-being of mankind.

On the next four pages you will find cutouts for 17 matching statements that illustrate the unique design of the universe.

- Cut out the boxes and distribute the slips of paper among the students. (Be sure you distribute an even number so that each statement has its matching conclusion).
- Instruct the students to find the person who has the statement that matches their own. Ask the newly formed pairs to stand together. (The process must be done silently. Hand signals are acceptable.)
- Once the pairs are standing together, ask them to read their facts to the group. The teacher can emphasize the facts as they are presented.

After the oral presentations are completed, direct the students to the facts that are asked for in their lesson. See if they can remember the answers from the oral presentation, and then have them write the facts in their lesson.

1A The earth is 8,000 miles in diameter and weighs roughly 6.6 x 10^{21} tons. It travels a 292 million–mile orbit around the sun.	1B If the earth traveled much faster, centrifugal force would pull it away from the sun; and if it were pulled away too far, all life would cease.
2A The earth's 365-day, 5-hour, 48-minute and 45.51-second round trip is accurate to a thousandth of a second.	2B If the earth traveled slightly slower, the earth would move closer to the sun; and if it moved too close, all life would perish.
3A If the yearly average temperature on earth rose or fell only a few degrees ...	3B Most life on earth would soon roast or freeze. This change would upset the balance of water and ice, and other balances, with disastrous results.

4A If the earth rotated on its axis slower …	4B All life would die in time, either by freezing at night because of lack of heat from the sun, or by burning during the day from too much sun.
5A If the moon were much nearer to earth …	5B Huge tides would overflow onto the lowlands and erode the mountains (and with the continents leveled, it is estimated that water would cover the entire surface of the earth to the depth of one and one-half miles.)
6A If the earth were not tilted 23 degrees on its axis, but were at a 90-degree angle in reference to the sun …	6B We would not have four seasons. Without seasons, life would soon not be able to exist here—the poles would lie in eternal twilight, and water vapor from the oceans would be carried by the wind towards both the north and south and would freeze when close enough to the poles. In time, huge continents of snow and ice would pile up in the polar regions, leaving most of the earth a dry desert. Eventually the oceans would disappear and rainfall would cease.
7A Water covers 70% of the earth's surface. Water is unique in that it absorbs large amounts of heat without much alteration in its temperature. If it were not for the tremendous amount of water on the earth …	7B There would be far greater day-and-night temperature variations. Many parts of the surface would be hot enough to boil water in the day and cool enough at night to freeze. The large oceans on earth are a vital part of our survival.

8A If cooled water did not stop contracting at 4 degrees centigrade and then *expand* until it froze (unlike most other substances) …	8B Then cool water would become heavier and sink to the bottom of the ocean. The ocean bottom would be extremely cold—and many fish would die. In time, more and more of the ocean would become ice.
9A Surface water after heating sinks to the bottom and warms the depth of the oceans and helps to produce ocean currents. If we didn't have ocean currents …	9B The ocean wouldn't stay in liquid form, and currents could not do many other things (such as distribute heat).
10A Unlike water, air rises after it is warmed. The air near the surface rises upward and maintains a temperature in which life can exist. If air acted the same way that water did …	10B The temperature on the earth's surface would be unbearable—and life could not survive for very long. The temperature a few hundred feet above the surface, on the other hand, would be quite cold and life could not exist.
11A Warm air rising upward creates air currents. If we did not have wind …	11B Then carbon dioxide would not be taken away from areas which overproduce it, and oxygen would not be moved to areas that need it.
12A The mixture of gases usually found in the atmosphere is perfect for life. If it were much different (more oxygen, less carbon dioxide, heavier atmospheric pressure, etc.) …	12B Life would cease to exist.

13A Regularities There are many laws that are consistent: they don't change. If we didn't have this regularity, we couldn't exist. If we couldn't be sure that space will be here tomorrow ...	13B Then we would wake up and disappear.
14A Regularities We can assume because of the law of gravity that gravity isn't going to change tomorrow. If it did ...	14B Then we would fly out of our beds and never come back again.
15A We have a three-dimensional universe. If we didn't	15B Then we couldn't exist. Atoms and molecules could not exist in two-, four- or other dimensional universes.
16A Electromagnetic force (the force that attracts positive and negative charges) is a constant strength in the universe. If it were a little bit weaker than it is ...	16B Then the electrons that are held around the nucleus of atoms by the electromagnetic force would fly off into space, and there would be no possibility of atoms' sharing electrons to make molecules. Without molecules, life isn't possible.
17A If the electromagnetic force were any stronger than it is ...	17B Then electrons would never move off its nucleus. They would be held so tightly that they would never be shared with other atoms. If electrons were never shared, molecules could not arise. Without molecules there is no life.

It All Begins With Genesis

LESSON 16

Recognizing different worldviews in science (part 2)

Scripture: 2 Peter 3:3–6; Genesis 7

Suggested memory verse:

2 Peter 3:5–6

What this lesson is about:

Lessons 15–19 contrast the naturalistic and biblical worldviews in the scientific areas of the origin of the universe, rocks and fossils, life and groups of life, and mankind. Today's lesson focuses on the two major ways of looking at the rocks and fossils of the earth. Challenging questions will be asked: Is it reasonable? Is it true? What does the eyewitness say? Which is compelling?

7 C's Connection: Catastrophe

Goals for the lesson: The student should

- understand the difference between *uniformitarianism* and *catastrophism*.
- understand the basics of the two ways that the geological column could have formed.
- see how fossils are formed.
- know what the eyewitness says concerning catastrophe in earth history.

Preparation for lesson:

- Work through the student's lesson 16.
- Props for lesson:

  Six illustrations/overheads introducing the two worldviews and fossils (available on the curriculum CD, labeled 16-1, 16-2, 16-3, 16-6, 16-7, 16-8)

  Two illustrations explaining the words 'uniformitarianism' (16-4) and 'catastrophism' (16-5) to place on the worldview bulletin board

  Photo or transparency showing sedimentary strata (e.g., Grand Canyon shot in illustration 16-1)

  Materials for fossil activity: blankets; coats; and signs for carnivores, scavengers, aerobic decomposers, and anaerobic decomposers

Materials for geological 'sandbox' activity:

Small disposable cups (6 oz)—9 blue and 9 red, clearly labeled with #1 Cambrian—uniformitarian, #1 Cambrian—catastrophic, etc.

Sugars—white, dark brown, light brown (fill cups 1, 4, 7 with white sugar; cups 2, 5, 8 with light brown sugar; and cups 3, 6, 9 with dark brown sugar (or use rice colored in different shades, stained with food coloring; or use different shades of sand).

If desired, bring some 'fossils'—raisins, with nuts in several of the cups; and bring two clear empty 2-liter bottles, such as used for Pepsi and Coke (find bottles that are clear all the way to the bottom; cut off the tops).

The script for the geological 'sandbox' activity is found on the next page. You will see two versions: simplified and detailed. The one you choose will depend on the educational level of the class and also the amount of time you have available for the activity.

- Additions to the worldview bulletin board, contrasting the two worldviews. Ask: Is it reasonable? What does the eyewitness say? Is it true?

Plan for lesson:

- **Introduction.** Show a photo or illustration of the sedimentary rocks of the earth, such as a picture of Grand Canyon (illustration 16-1). Ask students to think of a way that all this could be explained, if one did not believe in God or the claims of Scripture. Give them a few moments to think and write something down (section 1 in the student workbook).

- **Teach the uniformitarian view.** Put on your green naturalistic eyeglasses and tell the class that we will first consider the naturalistic worldview. You can present this worldview simply by reading the excerpt found in the lesson (section 2) or by asking what your students have learned from earth science class or museums.

  Ask, 'Is this a reasonable idea?' *(yes)* Then ask, 'Is there any other way of looking at it?' *(Yes, the catastrophic view. The choice is either a little bit of water over a lot of time OR a lot of water over a little bit of time.)*

  Show the illustrations of the two points of view (16-2, 16-3).

- **Teach**. You will now need to define uniformitarianism (16-4) and catastrophism (16-5) in section 3 of the student workbook.

  Uniformitarianism: The concept that geological processes occur by the action of natural laws that are always the same, and by processes that can be observed today (sediments that pile up where a small stream enters a river, erosion of a rock when water runs over it for a long time, etc.)

  Catastrophism: The theory that a significant portion of the geologic structure of the earth was formed in a global catastrophe of short duration—years rather than millions of years (biblical Flood).

- **Activity/Illustration: geological sandbox**

  1. On the table in front of you, arrange materials so that the uniformitarianism display is on your left, and the catastrophism display on the right. On your left you will have nine blue cups labeled Cambrian, Ordovician, etc. You will also have a 2-liter clear plastic container

ready to receive the uniformitarian deposits. Write 'naturalistic' on the container that will receive these deposits.

On the right will be nine red cups, also labeled Cambrian, Ordovician, etc., and a 2-liter clear plastic container ready to receive the catastrophic deposits. Label 'biblical' on that container.

When you finish depositing the cups into their containers, you will have two 'geologic columns' that look the same but have come about in two very different ways.

2. Refer students to the comparison sheet found in their lesson. Tell them that you will help them fill in the blanks as they go. Have materials on the table in front of the class. Invite two students to come forward to represent each view. It would be helpful to have a picture of the strata of Grand Canyon or of a schematic geological column in front of the class, and then when each system is introduced, put a sign or a punch pin on the layer being considered.

3. Begin with the Cambrian description, uniformitarian style. While you are reading the description, instruct the student to sprinkle the deposit slowly into the uniformitarian container. Next, read the Cambrian description, catastrophic style. Ask the other student to quickly dump the deposit into the catastrophic container. (Your 'uniformitarian' student will have to continue sprinkling while you go on to the catastrophic description, because he will take a long time.) Have the students fill in a comment on their own geologic column sheet to help them remember each description.

4. Proceed on through the sedimentary layers. Tell the group you are dealing only with layers that have been specifically identified as Flood deposits. Not all the geologic column represents the Flood. (Some of the column was formed by post-Flood catastrophes.) You want them to see that the same data (as listed in the center column of the chart) can be interpreted in two different ways.

5. When you complete the demonstration, ask:

   Are both of these interpretations of the data *reasonable*?
   Can they both be *right*?
   Which is more compelling to you and why?
   What does the eyewitness report say?

(Note: You may find that the students' attention span will not allow you to continue through all nine stratigraphic layers in the exercise. Do as many as time and their attention spans will allow.)

- **Activity: how to become a fossil.** You can illustrate this in a humorous fashion by inviting a student to volunteer to come up front. Tell the class that this student is very eager to be immortalized by someday becoming a fossil and occupying a special place in a museum. Tell them that you are going to show them how difficult it would be for the student to become a fossil. (Note: You might want to use illustration 16-6 on the curriculum CD.)

Step one: Avoid the carnivores that would get you *before* you die. (You could give several students signs identifying themselves as carnivores and let them march past the prospective 'fossil' student.)

Step two: If you manage to avoid the carnivores before you die, you must then avoid the scavengers after you die. (Difficult, because you are already dead.) (Have student lie down on floor—he is dead. Have one or more students hold 'scavenger' signs and walk by.)

Step three: Well, you've made it past the carnivores and scavengers. But now you must be buried *very* deeply, because the aerobic decomposers (fungi and bacteria) will make fast work of you if you are covered by only a foot or two of mud. (Cover student with someone's coat or a light sheet. Have one or more students with an 'aerobic decomposer' sign walk past.)

Step four: Even if you are buried very deeply, you still have a problem: anaerobic decomposers. These are slower but very efficient. (Pile some more coats or covers on top of the student to bury him more deeply. Then allow a student with an 'anaerobic decomposer' sign to walk past.)

Step five: You must be buried deeply and quickly, and the conditions must be right for lithification (the formation of rock). You would need water, certain chemicals and pressure. (Pour a small glass of water on the student, and 'step' on him for pressure.)

Step six: You must be able to get up to the surface again in order to be discovered before you erode away. (Let him come out from under the covers.) You see, you can't just die and fall down and become a fossil. So there shouldn't be very many fossils, right?

But ... fossils are abundant on the earth.

Ask. 'Which of the two views we talked about, *uniformitarianism* or *catastrophism*, would be the most likely to form many fossils?'

- **Class work.** Assign the following Scripture, as printed in their lesson:

  Genesis 7:11–12

  2 Peter 3:3–6

If you have additional time ...
Suggestions for augmenting lessons (home school, day school)

One or more extra sessions would be helpful. This class could be integrated with an earth science class, and the students could construct a stratigraphic column with the fossils known to be in the various layers. This could be an extended project in earth science. In any case, it would be helpful to divide the lesson into two: the first focusing on the rock column, the second focusing on fossils.

Answers in Genesis offers several supplemental resources, including the video *Grand Canyon: Monument to Catastrophe* as well as *The Fossil Book* and *Dry Bones* by Dr. Gary Parker and *Evolution Exposed: Earth Science* (all available from www.AnswersInGenesis.org).

The geological column–sedimentary strata

Uniformitarianism interpretation	Data (just the facts)	Catastrophism interpretation
Cup 1. Cambrian—This layer arose 500–570 million years ago. It took about 70 million years for this layer to be deposited. Many forms of sea creatures without backbones were evolving during this time: sponges, worms, crab-like creatures called arthropods, echinoderms (starfishes) and trilobites. **Summary:** Creatures without backbones evolved in the ocean 500 million years ago; it took 70 million years.	*Cambrian explosion* Variety of advanced forms of marine life; Various marine invertebrates, including trilobites and brachiopods (a shelled animal), worms, jellyfish, snails, sponges and cephalopods (similar to squid and octopus)	**Cup 1. Cambrian—**As the Flood began, new ocean currents began to transport and redeposit ocean sediments. The water was moving very fast. Many animals could not escape and were preserved as fossils. Many others did escape and were buried later. Many little invertebrate creatures burrowed around and lived in those sediments. These included trilobites. When you look at this first rock sequence, you see the marine organisms that lived in the ocean bottoms and were buried earliest in the Flood. **Summary:** Ocean-bottom creatures were buried earliest in the Flood.
Cup 2 Ordovician—This took place 435 million years ago. These layers took about 65 million years to be deposited. Shallow seas moved over the land and then retreated. Different sea creatures continued to evolve. Most still had no backbones. **Summary:** It took 65 million years for the evolution of sea creatures without backbones.	Brachiopods, snails, clams, mollusks, coral and early vertebrate fish	**Cup 2. Ordovician—**The Flood waters continue to advance. During the Flood, many invertebrate animals were moving around. They weren't all suddenly killed and buried. Many continued to live for a time and were able to burrow up through the sand. If there was a quiet period of time, even a few hours, the live animals would make burrows. If sediment accumulated over the burrow, some would try to burrow up through it, leaving escape burrows. Others would swim up in the water and come down on top of the next layer. **Summary:** Ocean-bottom creatures seeking to burrow to safety were covered in Flood sediments.

Uniformitarianism interpretation	Data (just the facts)	Catastrophism interpretation
Cup 3. Silurian—It took place about 408 million years ago. These layers took 30 million years to be deposited. The first fish with jaws evolved and the first land insects evolved. A few fish with backbones evolved. **Summary:** The evolution of the first fish with jaws and the first land insects took place over a period of 30 million years.	Marine life— invertebrate and vertebrate; echinoderms (starfish relatives); spiders and millipedes on land; land plants	**Cup 3. Silurian—**The Flood waters continued to rise and sediments came in quickly. Armored fish are bottom-dwelling fish; other fish can hide from danger on the sea floor. These would then be the first vertebrate ('with backbone') fish to be buried, as a sudden influx of sediment came in. Wow, look at that sediment coming in so quickly and burying all those fish! **Summary:** Fish with backbones who dwelt near the bottom were buried under sediment.
Cup 4. Devonian—It happened 360 million years ago. These layers took 53 million years to be deposited. Continents collided in this era, resulting in great mountain building. During this time the first air-breathing arthropods (spiders and mites) evolved on dry land. In the seas, coiled shellfish called ammonoids evolved. Devonian fish had fins, scales and jaws. They developed into the first air-breathing vertebrate life (amphibians), and they invaded the land at the end of this period. **Summary:** Over a period of 53 million years, spiders evolved on dry land; amphibians also began to evolve.	Bony fishes and amphibians; large land plants, such as horsetails, ferns and cone-bearing plants	**Cup 4. Devonian—**The floodwaters continued to rise. Here come more sediments, and the little amphibians and reptiles just can't escape them any longer! Many amphibians and reptiles were also active, leaving footprints during the middle part of the Flood. The Appalachian mountains were formed early in the Flood. (This explains why they had an opportunity to erode more than the Rockies, in the late Mesozoic.) **Summary:** Little amphibians and reptiles could no longer escape the floodwaters.

Uniformitarianism interpretation	Data (just the facts)	Catastrophism interpretation
Cup 5. Carboniferous—This is still part of the Paleozoic era. It happened 290 million years ago. These rocks took 70 million years to be deposited. During this time lush forests and tropical peat swamps from which coal, oil and gas would form covered large areas. Much evolution of plant life. The first sea reptiles evolved, as did corals, crinoids (like sea lillies), foraminifers (like protozoans) and snails and mollusks. Sharks and brachiopods were present. **Summary:** Over 70 million years, plant life went through abundant evolution. Sea reptiles, sharks and snails also evolved.	Coal and oil deposits; amphibians and fish; crinoids; insects, such as giant cockroaches and dragonflies; reptiles (large lizards)	**Cup 5. Carboniferous—**The floodwaters continued to advance, and the lowland swampy areas alongside the oceans were covered with sediments. The lowland life zones were covered. The swamps were populated with plants, amphibians and reptiles. There might have been floating plants that grew in water. Fossil vertebrate footprints are common in middle and upper Paleozoic deposits, indicating that the animals were quite active on the new sediments before they were killed or buried. **Summary:** Lowland swampy areas were covered by sediments of the Flood: burial of plants, amphibians, water-dwelling reptiles.
Cup 6. Permian—It took place until 240 million years ago and lasted for 50 million years. These rocks are rich in deposits of coal, oil and gas. This was a time of widespread crustal unrest, with continents being raised and mountain ranges being formed. All of earth's landmasses united into one enormous mass, called Pangaea. The earth saw the evolution of different kinds of trees and many more forms of reptiles and amphibians. **Summary:** 50 million years of evolution saw more tree evolution and the evolution of early dinosaur types.	Reptiles and amphibians increasing, death of many marine species	**Cup 6. Permian—**Water currents were affecting amphibians and small reptiles, as they could no longer escape. They would climb up the sides of the dunes against the current, trying to escape, but they were buried. Lots of amphibians or reptiles left their footprints on cross-bedded sandstones, where we can see them today. **Summary:** Strong water currents buried amphibians and small reptiles.

Uniformitarianism interpretation	Data (just the facts)	Catastrophism interpretation
Cup 7. Triassic—This is considered to be the first of the era that is called Mesozoic ('middle-life'). This period took place until 205 million years ago. The rocks took 35 million years to be deposited. During the Triassic period, the supercontinent Pangaea began tearing apart. The climate was warm and evergreen trees dominated the terrain. Many dinosaurs evolved during this time, and small mammals were evolving. **Summary:** 35 million years. Dinosaurs appeared, and the first true mammals evolved.	Dinosaurs in all sizes; lush forests of cone-bearing trees and cycads (like modern palm trees); ichthyosaurs and plesiosaurs in oceans; ammonite (shellfish like the modern nautilus)	**Cup 7. Triassic—**As the Flood continued, its waters encountered other life zones. Mesozoic deposits contain the remains from pre-Flood lowlands dominated by dinosaurs and other large reptiles. Perhaps they were not found in earlier sediments because they lived inland from the swamps. They also may have been more mobile and could escape farther. **Summary:** Waters invade lowlands dominated by dinosaurs and other large reptiles. These probably lived inland from swamps and were more mobile.
Cup 8. Jurassic—This is the second division of the Mesozoic era. This took place until about 144 million years ago. These rocks took about 64 million years to be deposited. The Jurassic climate was warm and moist. Reptiles were the dominant form of animal life and had adapted to life in the sea (ichthyosaurs and plesiosaurs), in the air (pterosaurs), and on the land, where some reached huge sizes (*Allosaurus* and *Apatosaurus*). Mammals remained small and rodent-like. **Summary:** 64 million years. Very large dinosaurs evolved. Small mammals such as rats evolved.	Dinosaurs dominant—saurischians, *Stegosaurus*; flying reptiles (pterosaurs); tiny mammals (rodent-like creatures); *Archaeopteryx* bird	**Cup 8. Jurassic—**As the Flood progressed, other animals were affected. These included swimming reptiles, such as plesiosaurs and ichthyosaurs, and flying reptiles, or pterosaurs. The first mammals and birds to be buried were all small—the size of mice or rats. **Summary:** As the Flood progressed, swimming and flying reptiles were buried, as well as some birds and small mammals, such as rats.

Uniformitarianism interpretation	Data (just the facts)	Catastrophism interpretation
Cup 9. Cretaceous—This is the last time period of the Mesozoic era. It took place until 65 million years ago. These rocks took about 73 million years to be deposited. During the late Cretaceous, sea levels rose worldwide, eventually producing a warm, mild global climate. Many of today's trees were present. The Rocky Mountains and the Sierra Nevada were uplifted at this time. **Summary:** Over 73 million years, many modern trees evolved; dinosaurs disappeared.	Dinosaurs, including *Tyrannosaurus;* flowering plants (angiosperms); trees; mass extinction of many species, including all dinosaurs	**Cup 9. Cretaceous—**These animals seem to represent two groups: animals that could escape the floodwaters longer than the others, or animals that lived at higher elevations. The plants were those in the cooler, upland environments. The Rocky Mountains uplifted during this part of the Flood. **Summary:** Plants and animals in cooler, upland environments were buried.

Simplified column illustration

Uniformitarian interpretation	Catastrophism interpretation
Cup 1 *(Cambrian—assigned to the 'Paleozoic era'; lowest layer; filled with sea creatures without backbones, such as trilobites, worms, shelled animals, jellyfish, snails, and squid- or octopus-like creatures)* These layers took 500 million years to form, as life was evolving in the ocean.	**Cup 1** *(Cambrian—assigned to the 'Paleozoic' era; lowest layer; filled with sea creatures without backbones, such as trilobites, worms, shelled animals, jellyfish, and snails)* Creatures that lived on the ocean bottom were buried earliest in the Flood. These were types of marine organisms that lived at the time of the Flood.
Cup 2 *(Ordovician; Paleozoic 'era'; more sea creatures without backbones—clams, snails, coral; some fish with backbones)* This layer formed about 436 million years ago. It took about 65 million years for these sea creatures to evolve.	**Cup 2** *(Ordovician; Paleozoic 'era'; more sea creatures without backbones—clams, snails, coral; some fish with backbones)* This layer shows what happened as the floodwaters continued to advance. Many invertebrate animals (creatures without backbones) were moving around and burrowed to find a way of escape. As they were scurrying away, they were covered in Flood sediments.
Cup 3 *(Silurian; Paleozoic; more marine life, both with and without backbones; starfish; some spiders and land insects; land plants)* These layers took 30 million years to be deposited. They show the evolution of the first fish with jaws and the first land insects.	**Cup 3** *(Silurian; Paleozoic; more marine life, both with and without backbones; starfish; some spiders and land insects; land plants)* Fish with backbones who dwelt near the bottom of the ocean were the next to be buried under the sediments of the Flood.
Cup 4 *(Devonian; Paleozoic; more bony fishes, amphibians, and large land plants, such as ferns)* These layers took 53 million years to form. Spiders evolved on dry land; and amphibians, which could go on dry land or in the water, also began to evolve.	**Cup 4** *(Devonian; Paleozoic; more bony fishes, amphibians, and large land plants, such as ferns)* The little amphibians and reptiles could no longer escape the floodwaters, so they were buried in these layers.
Cup 5 *(Carboniferous; Paleozoic; coal and oil; amphibians and fish; giant cockroaches and dragonflies; reptiles, such as large lizards)* These rocks took 70 million years to be deposited. In the lush forests and swamps of this era, plant life, such as ferns, was evolving. Evolution of sea reptiles and sharks.	**Cup 5** *(Carboniferous; Paleozoic; coal and oil; amphibians and fish; giant cockroaches and dragonflies; reptiles, such as large lizards)* Now the Flood waters have advanced to the lowland swampy areas alongside the oceans. These swamps were populated with ferns, amphibians and water-dwelling reptiles. They left lots of footprints, an indication that they were quite active before they were killed or buried.

Uniformitarian interpretation	Catastrophism interpretation
Cup 6 *(Permian; Paleozoic era; reptiles and amphibians; not as many ocean species)* These layers represent 50 million years of evolution. Mountains were forming and land coming together. More trees evolved. Forerunners of dinosaurs evolved.	**Cup 6** *(Permian; Paleozoic era; reptiles and amphibians, not as many ocean species)* Very strong water currents buried amphibians and small reptiles. Lots of them left their footprints on sandstone 'dunes,' which we can see today.
Cup 7 *(Triassic; Mesozoic era; dinosaurs; lush forests of cone-bearing trees; ichthyosaurs and plesiosaurs in oceans)* These rocks took 35 million years to be deposited. Dinosaurs first appeared. They would later become larger. Some true mammals began to evolve.	**Cup 7** *(Triassic; Mesozoic 'era'; dinosaurs; lush forests of cone-bearing trees; ichthyosaurs and plesiosaurs in oceans)* As the Flood continued, its waters encountered other life zones. These deposits contain the remains from pre-Flood lowlands dominated by dinosaurs and other large reptiles. They lived more inland from the swamps. They also may have been more mobile and could escape farther.
Cup 8 *(Jurassic; Mesozoic; large dinosaurs, rodent-like mammals,* Archaeopteryx *bird)* These sediments took 64 million years to be deposited (about 144–200 million years ago). Very large dinosaurs evolved. Small mammals, such as rats, evolved.	**Cup 8** *(Jurassic; Mesozoic; large dinosaurs, rodent-like mammals,* Archaeopteryx *bird)* As the Flood progressed, swimming and flying reptiles were buried, as well as some birds and small mammals, such as rats.
Cup 9 *(Cretaceous; Mesozoic; dinosaurs; flowering plants (angiosperms), many dinosaurs no longer seen)* These sediments took 73 million years to be deposited. In the mild global climate, many of today's kinds of trees evolved. Many kinds of dinosaurs became extinct. The Rocky Mountains and the Sierra Nevada were uplifted at this time.	**Cup 9** *(Cretaceous; Mesozoic; dinosaurs; flowering plants (angiosperms), many dinosaurs no longer seen)* These fossils seem to represent either animals that could escape the floodwaters longer than the others or organisms that lived at higher elevations. The plants buried were those in the cooler, upland environments. The Rocky Mountains uplifted during this part of the Flood.

It All Begins With Genesis

LESSON 17

Recognizing different worldviews in science (part 3)

Scripture: Job 12:7–10; Colossians 1:16; Nehemiah 9:6

Suggested memory verse:

Nehemiah 9:6b

What this lesson is about:

Lessons 15–19 contrast the naturalistic and biblical worldviews in the scientific areas of the origin of the universe, rocks and fossils, life and groups of life, and mankind. Today's lesson focuses on the two major ways of looking at the origin of life. The 'simple' cell and the proteins and DNA within will be discussed. Challenging questions will be asked of each worldview: Is it reasonable? Is it true? What does the eyewitness say? Is it compelling?

7 C's Connection: Creation

Goals for the lesson: The student should

- be able to describe—in a simple way—how the two worldviews believe the first living cell came to be.
- recognize evidence for intelligent design when he sees it.
- begin to grasp the incredible complexity and intelligent design in a 'simple' cell.
- increase in his critical ability to think and evaluate both the presuppositions and the message communicated by Scripture.

Preparation for lesson:

- Work through the student's lesson 17.
- Props needed:

  Worldview glasses
  Actual arrowhead and natural stone, if available
  Seven various illustrations (on the curriculum CD)
  String of colored beads to represent amino acids in a protein
  Playing cards
  Descriptions of the parts of the 'cell spaceship,' placed in sealed envelopes on the wall in front of the room (pages T-99 and T-100)
  Cut-up parts of the cell, one set for each student (at the end of this lesson)
  Tape
  Glue
  Marker for overheads

Plan for lesson:

- **Introduction.** Show a photo of living things (or use 17-1 on the CD). Ask how living things could have come to be. Ask students to think of a way that even the simplest of living things could be explained if one did not believe in God or the claims of Scripture. Give them a few minutes to think and write something down, and then give them a brief opportunity to share what they wrote.

- **Teach.** Put on the naturalistic eyeglasses. Use the illustration 'Naturalism would say…' (17-2) to teach the naturalistic worldview. Read the quote from the biology book given on the illustration. Ask, 'Is this reasonable?' *(yes, if you don't believe in God)* Then ask, 'Is there another way of looking at it? Could something like this really happen by time, chance and natural processes?' (Use illustration 17-3.)

- **Illustrate.** Show the students an arrowhead and a river stone. Ask if they can tell any difference between the two. One was designed (by a human), and natural water processes formed the other. Point out that it is very easy for anyone to differentiate things that are designed and things that are not. (You can use other examples, such as a building, a wristwatch, etc.)

- **Airplane illustration.** Ask students to think about a Boeing 747 and what makes it fly. Can aluminum fly? Can the engine fly? etc. Point out that a Boeing 747 is a collection of 4½ million non-flying parts. Ask: What makes it fly? Answer: intelligent design. Then bring up the cell—it is a collection of several billion non-living molecules. What makes it live?

- **Mind-boggler illustration: DNA.** Tell students you want to 'boggle their mind' for a few minutes. Read each statement on illustration 17-4 separately (cover up the other parts of the illustration). Help them digest each statement. (For example, when you read the first statement about DNA, put a little period on the board to illustrate that the entire DNA is spelled out in that one pinhead point.)

- **Mind-boggler illustration: proteins.** Again, take it one statement at a time on illustration 17-5. When you finish reading the information, illustrate further using a string of colored plastic beads. Again reinforce that each must be in exact order, and that the average protein has 400 of these amino acids to arrange in order.

  Bring out your playing cards. Deal out 17 cards face up to students (in small groups, if you have a large number of students). Designate someone in each group to put the cards back, mix them up and deal them out again. Tell them you want to see how long it will take them to deal the same 17 cards in the same order again. Ask them to guess how long that would take for the same 17 cards to come up again. Answer: 355 trillion times (have someone write it on the board).

  (This information is from *The Amazing Story of Creation* by Duane Gish, p. 33.) Now point out that if you had a protein with 100 amino acids in its chain, the probability of lining up in that order again is one followed by 130 zeros. (Have someone write that on the board.)

Finally, when you finish, you only have one dead protein. Look again at the protein illustration about the many thousands of proteins needed in the cell. And still, proteins are dead molecules. What makes life?

- **'Parts of the cell' activity**

Preparation. On page T-101 you will find two sets of small labels for each part of the cell. Each student will need a set of these labels. (Photocopy as many labels as you need, and cut them out.) Students will also need glue sticks.

On pages T-99 and T-100 are detailed descriptions of several parts of the cell. Cut out the descriptions and place each in a separate envelope. Tape the envelopes in a conspicuous place where they can be used during the lesson.

You also need to enlarge a copy of the cell diagram (17-6, available on the CD) that the students have in their workbooks. You may project it as a transparency or PowerPoint image, or create a poster.

Activity. You might introduce the activity as follows: 'Now let's consider one "simple" cell. In Darwin's day it was believed that a cell was just a blob of protoplasm, so it seemed reasonable that it could have evolved from chemicals. Now we know that the cell isn't simple at all—it is another mind-boggler.'

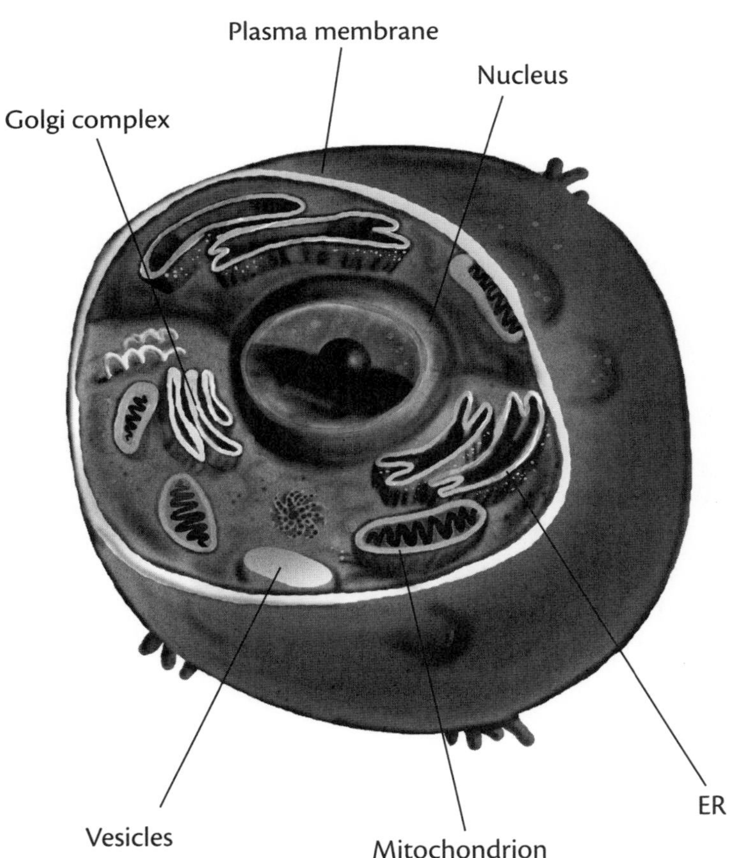

Ask the students to think of the cell as a huge spaceship the size of New York City. Then hand out glue sticks and the six parts of the cell. Tell them that they will look at just a few parts of the spaceship. When they understand each part they have in their hands, they will place it in the proper space on the cell in their lesson.

You can invite students who wish to participate to come up one at a time and remove an envelope from the wall and read about that part of the 'spaceship.' You will probably have to reinforce what they have read. Then on the illustration, have students help you find and mark the part just explained. Then have them glue the appropriate part on the cell diagram.

- **Summary illustration: two worldviews.** Ask students which worldview is compelling. Bring out that this is just one cell—so incredibly complex that we can't even begin to understand it fully. And our body has hundreds of different kinds of cells. What is required here? (They should easily see that it requires intelligence beyond anything we can imagine.)
- **What does the eyewitness say? Discussion time in small groups.** The students should study the Scripture given in their lesson and answer the questions about each passage. As you conclude the class, ask them to share one thing they learned from the lesson today. You could also ask what they learn about God from what He has made.

If you have additional time ...
Suggestions for augmenting lessons (home school, day school)

One or more extra sessions would be helpful. This class can be integrated with a life science or biology class, including extra study on DNA, proteins and the cell.

Answers in Genesis has several resources, including the video *The Origin of Life, The New Answers Book 2 (chapter 6) and Evolution Exposed: Biology (chapter 5)* (available from www.AnswersIn-Genesis.org).

Unlocking the Mystery of Life (DVD) is an excellent resource for demonstrating the incredible complexity of life. It uses computer animation to transport the viewer into the interior of the living cell to explore systems and machines that bear the unmistakable hallmarks of design. It runs for 65 minutes, but you could select portions of the program for class viewing. This video can also be ordered from www.AnswersInGenesis.org

Activity: parts of the cell

You may wish to highlight only part of the description and instruct the students to read that part, if you are having trouble keeping their attention.

- **Plasma membrane.** This is the wall of the spaceship. It is like the skin on a balloon. It has doors that open and close unexpectedly, with an army of guards controlling who comes in and out. This membrane protects the cell. There are proteins everywhere: some in various places, others moving along the membrane. These proteins tell the cell what is outside and control what enters and exits. It is also like a workbench. Proteins are built on those membranes, and chemical reactions take place.
- **Nucleus.** This is the control center of the spaceship, where the captain rides and directs the activity of the ship. It is normally round or oval and usually in the middle of the cell.

  In the nucleus is **DNA.** This is like a twisted rope ladder. It contains much of the information that runs the cell and is like the blueprints or operation manuals of a spaceship. It has billions of parts. It is a language that has the information needed to build proteins. It can unwrap itself, unzip itself and copy itself in just minutes.

  Also in the nucleus is the *nucleolus.* It is the place where *ribosomes* are made. Ribosomes are like the building foreman who reads the blueprints and tells others how to build the building or spaceship. They act as assembly lines, taking sections of information copied off DNA and connecting a precise sequence of amino acids in a certain way to make the proteins (or individual parts) needed by the cell (or spaceship).
- **Endoplasmic reticulum (ER).** This is like the factory or manufacturing part of the cell. The ER consists of folded membranes around the nucleus. Part of it looks like big tubes that have been mashed. All along the membrane are proteins called enzymes. These are special proteins that speed up chemical reactions.

  On the flattened sections of the ER are dots. The dots are the ribosomes that were made in the nucleolus to read the DNA. Most of the proteins of the cell are made in the ER.
- **Golgi complex. The 'post office' or shipping department of the spaceship.** The Golgi complex looks like a stack of different sized pita breads. Since proteins are made in one place and have to work in other places, they have to be moved around. When proteins are made in the cell, they are sent to the Golgi complex. The Golgi complex takes the different proteins inside it, sorts them and sends them to the correct part of the cell.
- **Vesicles. Delivery service—UPS trucks of the spaceship.** Proteins are moved through the cell in little membrane sacs called vesicles. Vesicles can form off the surface of a membrane, just like you can blow a bubble off a sheet of bubble film. When the protein is formed in the ER, a vesicle forms around it as it leaves. The vesicle travels to the Golgi complex. It bumps into the side of the Golgi complex and then melts into it, putting the protein inside the Golgi complex. It moves through the Golgi complex and then leaves in another vesicle and is sent to where it needs to go.

- **Mitochondrion. Power plant of the spaceship.** A mitochondrion has two layers of membrane. On the outside, a mitochondrion looks kind of like a bean. But if you cut past the membrane on the outside of the mitochondrion, you find another membrane. This one isn't smooth like the other. It is folded so that a lot of it can fit inside the first membrane. It needs extra space because a lot of work takes place on the second membrane.

  Mitochondria are like the power plants for the cell. They take energy from food molecules to make special molecules called ATP. ATP is very fragile and can only hold together for a very short time before part of it breaks off. When the part breaks off, though, it releases energy that the cell uses. ATP is always being made and used in every one of your cells. The ATP is made in a mitochondrion. Then it goes from the mitochondrion to just where it is needed. Then it breaks and releases the energy so that the cell can use it.

Wall of spaceship

(plasma membrane)

Doors that open and close, with guards controlling what comes in and out. Many different protein helpers. Protects the cell spaceship.

Wall of spaceship

(plasma membrane)

Doors that open and close, with guards controlling what comes in and out. Many different protein helpers. Protects the cell spaceship.

Control center of ship (nucleus)

This is where captain directs activity of the ship. DNA contains much information that runs the cell. It has billions of parts and is like the blueprint to make the thousands of proteins for the cell. Ribosomes are produced here. They read the blueprints and act as assembly lines to make the proteins needed.

Control center of ship (nucleus)

This is where captain directs activity of the ship. DNA contains much information that runs the cell. It has billions of parts and is like the blueprint to make the thousands of proteins for the cell. Ribosomes are produced here. They read the blueprints and act as assembly lines to make the proteins needed.

Manufacturing center of cell (endoplasmic reticulum—ER)

Looks like big tubes that have been mashed. All along it are special proteins called enzymes that speed up chemical reactions. Ribosomes that were made in the nucleus are found here doing their jobs in reading the DNA. Most of the proteins of the spaceship (cell) are made here.

Manufacturing center of cell (endoplasmic reticulum—ER)

Looks like big tubes that have been mashed. All along it are special proteins called enzymes that speed up chemical reactions. Ribosomes that were made in the nucleus are found here doing their jobs in reading the DNA. Most of the proteins of the spaceship (cell) are made here.

Post office/Shipping department (Golgi complex)

Since proteins are made in one place and have to work in other places, they have to be moved around. Once proteins are made, they are sent to the Golgi complex. The Golgi complex sorts them and sends them to the correct part of the cell.

Post office/Shipping department (Golgi complex)

Since proteins are made in one place and have to work in other places, they have to be moved around. Once proteins are made, they are sent to the Golgi complex. The Golgi complex sorts them and sends them to the correct part of the cell.

Delivery trucks of ship (vesicles)

Proteins are moved through the cell in little membrane sacs called vesicles. The vesicle travels to the Golgi complex, where it picks up the needed protein and then leaves in another vesicle to deliver the protein to where it needs to go.

Delivery trucks of ship (vesicles)

Proteins are moved through the cell in little membrane sacs called vesicles. The vesicle travels to the Golgi complex, where it picks up the needed protein and then leaves in another vesicle to deliver the protein to where it needs to go.

Power plant of spaceship (mitochondrion)

Mitochondria take energy from food molecules to make special molecules called ATP. ATP releases energy that the cell uses.

Power plant of spaceship (mitochondrion)

Mitochondria take energy from food molecules to make special molecules called ATP. ATP releases energy that the cell uses.

It All Begins With Genesis — LESSON 18

Recognizing different worldviews in science (part 4)

Life: the many varieties of living things

Scripture: Romans 1:18–20; Genesis 1:20–25; 1 Corinthians 15:39

Suggested memory verse:

Romans 1:20

What this lesson is about:

Lessons 15–19 contrast the naturalistic and Biblical worldviews in the scientific areas of the origin of the universe, rocks and fossils, life and groups of life, and mankind. Today's lesson focuses on the two major ways of looking at the origin of the major groups of living things. Questions were asked: Is it reasonable? Is it true? What does the eyewitness say? Which is compelling?

7 C's Connection: Creation

Goals for the lesson: The student should

- be able to describe—in a simple way—how the two worldviews believe the major groups of living creatures came to be.
- understand that the reason we are studying science in this way is to help know God better by knowing Him as Creator.
- increase in his critical ability to think and evaluate both the presuppositions behind the two views and the message communicated by Scripture.

Preparation for lesson:

- Work through the student's lesson 18.
- Props needed: book, worldview eyeglasses, four illustrations (found on the curriculum CD), pieces for scramble games (cutouts at the end of this lesson)
- Prepare a sign to add to the bulletin board contrasting the two worldviews.

Plan for lesson:

- **Introduction.** Last week we studied something about the 'simple cell.' What did you learn about how 'simple' it is?

  (Use illustration 18-1—'How did all the major groups of life come to be?') This week we will consider another question about living things: Assuming we have the 'simple' life, how can it be in so many different forms—octopus, snail, frangipani tree, raccoon, butterfly? If you didn't believe in God as Creator, how might you explain this diversity? (Don't take time to have students write down their answers.)

Teach. (Use illustration 18-2—'Origin of major groups of life: naturalism would say.') Read the explanation that was taken from a biology book.

It would be helpful here to clarify the definition of evolution. You could ask, 'If someone asked you if you believe in evolution, what should you say?' Answer: 'What do you mean by the word "evolution"?'

Discuss the different ways evolution is defined. (It can simply mean 'change.' It is also often used in reference to the *recombination* of genes. But we see this type of change all of the time, and it is not a problem for the Biblical worldview. The most common understanding of the word, however, is a change from one major kind into another ('goo to you' or 'fish to philosopher'). This form of evolution requires the creation of completely *new* information in the genes—something that scientists have never observed. This is the meaning of evolution that we are addressing here.

Point out from illustration 18-2 how evolution is supposed to occur. Write the following three terms on the board and tell students that they will be looking at each process to see if they can indeed cause evolution.

- *Genetic recombination* (Genetic information can be combined in new ways to produce more variation in a species.)
- *Mutations* (Mistakes can occur in the process of copying DNA information.)
- *Natural selection* (The individuals in a population that are best able to survive and reproduce in their environment will pass on more of their genes to succeeding generations than other individuals.)

- Next teach the Biblical worldview (use illustration 18-3—'Origin of major groups of life: biblical worldview would say'). You've already studied something about the different *baramins*, or 'created kinds.' The basic idea is that God created various 'kinds,' and within each was built in different genetic material to allow much change within each 'kind.'
- Teach next the concept of information. Show students a book (Bible or phone book). Tell them, 'Here is a Bible. It is full of lots of information. What kind of information do you find in the Bible? *(information about God, history of Israel, how to live, etc.)* Where is the information? Is it in the book cover? The paper? The letters on the page? If you were a Russian and didn't know our language, could you understand the information inside? What do you need? *(a code created by a mind. Mind is the secret to information.)*

Ask students what is the real information in smoke signals, Morse code, computers, etc. The main point you want them to see is that information is not a physical thing—it is created by a mind and involves a code of some kind.

The last item on the illustration is DNA, the most complicated code of all. Consider together what kind of mind is required to come up with the code for life (intelligence beyond anything humans can have).

- Now let's go back to the naturalistic explanation for evolution, how new groups of life are formed (illustration 18-2). Begin with the one-celled amoeba and point out the complex codes that have to be present to allow the amoeba to live, digest, reproduce. Then go to fish and ask students to tell you what fish need to be coded that amoeba don't need (gills, lungs, swimming, scales, eggs, eyes). What about squirrels? (fur, legs, tail, teeth) Birds? (feathers, wings, flight) Horses? (legs, hooves, mane, large heart) Man? (brain, speech, fingers and thumb)
- **Illustrate.** Refer again to the board. Now we need to look at the explanation for the way that evolution takes place and see if it is possible to obtain increased information by these three mechanisms.

  Scramble games: (Use as many as time allows. The cutouts are found at the end of this lesson.)

  Blue eyes/brown eyes. Give each child a slip of paper. It will have BB, Bb or bb. You might want to give the blue-eyed children the bb slips of paper, and distribute the rest of the slips randomly. Then ask the children with the bb's to go to one side of the room, the children with the BB's to go to the other side, and the children with the Bb's to go to the middle. Show them that this is simply genetic recombination. Each one of us receives two genes for eye color, one from our father and one from our mother. The large B (for brown) is dominant, so everyone who has BB or bB or Bb will have brown eyes. The only way to have blue or green eyes is to have two small b's—recessive genes. Point out that those who have bb have actually *lost* information. They will never be able to have brown-eyed children unless they marry someone who has the large B gene. The same is true for those who have the two BB's for brown. They could never have blue-eyed children. Conclude with this question: 'Can passing around these genes *add* information?' No!

  Dogs. The slips of paper have medium dogs, tiny dogs and large dogs. Have the medium dogs stay in the middle and the large and small dogs go to the side. Explain that the original dogs that came off the Ark were probably light brown animals weighing about 30 lb and endowed with an incredibly large and variable gene pool for size, color, length of hair, etc., so that they could adapt to and fit in any new environment they might encounter in the post-Flood world. Purebred dog breeders utilizing the large gene pool can, by artificial selection, select for the traits they desire. Eventually a large dog like a Saint Bernard can be produced. The variable gene pool has now been expanded to its limit. While the gene pool is very large, it is finite. Breeders cannot breed dogs to the size of large horses. Our biggest, strongest dog is still a dog and has only dog DNA, but he has *lost* some of his original dog genes. Lost forever from the Saint Bernard's gene pool are all the genes for cute little dogs. Also lost are some health traits. Now a large Saint Bernard may not be able to fight off some infectious diseases as well as the original mongrel dog. He may have frequent hip dysplasias or other congenital disorders. His gene pool is now much less complex, much less able to adapt to new environments or new diseases. *No* new information for new traits has been added—and that is essential for true upward evolution to occur.

  Peppered moths. The students will receive slips of paper for either light-colored moths or dark-colored moths. The peppered moth example is given in most biology textbooks as an example of evolution (although the story has now been discredited—see Paul Taylor's "An Examination of Error" in *Answers* magazine, July–September 2006 available online at www.AnswersMagazine.com). Let's see what would really have been happening here.

Have all the students stand up at their seats. Tell them that once upon a time in England, there were two different varieties of peppered moths: black and white. At that time, most of the tree bark in the area was whitish, with some lichens (also white) on them. Ask them which moths would be the easiest for birds to see and eat if the moths rested on the trees (the black ones). Now tell most of the children who have black slips of paper to sit down because they have just been eaten. A few dark moths would survive, but most of the survivors would be white moths. This is an example of natural selection.

Now pretend the industrial revolution came, trees were covered in dark soot and the white lichens on the tree disappeared. Now what color of moths would survive? Tell the white moths to sit down. The black ones would remain standing and would breed, and soon the majority of the population of moths would be black.

Ask the children if any new genetic information was produced? This is an example of change within a created kind; it happens all the time. It is simple genetic recombination and natural selection. The moths all simply remain moths. Could this process produce beetles? Butterflies? Yet this story is given as an example of 'fish-to-philosopher' evolution in almost every biology textbook.

Mosquitoes. The children will be either normal mosquitoes or super mosquitoes. The super mosquitoes have something in their genetic structure that makes them unable to metabolize (break down) a certain chemical. Have the children stand by their seats. Spray the room with DDT (figuratively, of course). The normal mosquitoes will die and sit down. The super mosquitoes will survive. This is *natural selection* in action. If the super mosquitoes have a chance to breed, you now have a swamp full of super mosquitoes. Go through the motion of spraying with DDT again. Ask what will happen. They will all be resistant to DDT. Is this evolution? *(no)* Was any new information added to the mosquito? *(No, actually there was less because this kind of mosquito was unable to metabolize a certain chemical.)*

Melanin in skin. Some children will have black skin (MM), some will have shades of brown (Mm) and some will have very light skin (mm). Teach the children that skin color in humans is determined simply by how much of a particular pigment—melanin—is present. Ask the children to form in three groups: white on one side, brown in the middle and dark on the other. This illustrates how *genetic recombination* can work. You could then point out that *natural selection* could come in here, too. For example, if the very white people moved to equatorial climates, they would encounter sun poisoning and melanomas. The very black people who moved to extreme northern areas with little direct sunlight could suffer from the inability to produce enough vitamin D. Is this evolution? *(no)* Is there any new information added? *(no)*

Now we'll give some examples of *mutations* because this (natural selection working on mutations) is the major reason given to explain evolution today.

Define 'mutations' as 'accidents that happen as a result of DNA copying.' Now we need to see if these accidents can help to further evolution—if they add helpful information. You can point out that most mutations are lethal or at least harmful to the organism.

Sickle-cell anemia. Some children will have sickle-cell mutation. The others have normal red blood cells. Ask all of the children to stand up. Tell them that the sickle-cell gene, if combined with someone else who has it, will produce anemia that will eventually kill them. Have the sickle-cell people sit down. Is this a helpful mutation?

You might point out that this example is often given in the textbooks as an example of a helpful mutation, because those who have the sickle-cell gene are immune from the disease malaria. For those who live in malaria-infested regions, the mutation is therefore helpful. But it is still a defect.

Beetles with and without wings. Some children will be beetles with wings and others will have a mutation and will not have wings. Ask all the children to stand at their seats. Tell them a bunch of birds are coming along to eat them. The ones who don't have wings will be unable to leave and will die. (Have that group sit down.) This is an example of natural selection.

But could having no wings be a 'good' mutation? Ask all the students to stand again. Tell them they live on a very windy island in the middle of the ocean. A huge wind comes along and blows the beetles with wings into the ocean. (Have those students sit down.) In this environment, the mutation for no wings would be a helpful kind of mutation to have.

But is this evolution? Can it go upward to bigger, more complex beetles and then to other things?

Fish with and without eyes. Some children are normal fish and others have a mutation for no eyes. Have them all stand up. Present the normal situation for fish with no eyes: they will not be able to escape predators and will be eaten. Have them sit down.

Ask, 'Is there any time that mutation might be beneficial? What if you were in a cave and didn't need to see?' The fish with no eyes would not be in danger of scraping those eyes on sharp rocks in the cave and would have an advantage over the ones with eyes. Natural selection would favor the fish with no eyes, and eyeless cave fish would multiply.

Is this evolution? Is there new information that will advance evolution upward?

- **Sum it up.** Use illustration 18-4—'Origin of major groups of life.' There are two ways of looking at it. Which is compelling? What does the eyewitness say?

- **The eyewitness.** Direct the class to section 5 on the second page of their lesson for today: Why are we studying 'science' in Sunday school? Have them read and answer the question for themselves. Then discuss each answer.

  a. No, we never want to 'bug' our science teachers. We do want to be able to ask thoughtful questions respectfully, but we must remember that we represent Christ and should do it politely.

  b. No, we aren't in it to debate. We do want to be able to know the truth and to discuss facts we know, but winning arguments is not what we're about.

  c. No, we don't need to prove that the Bible is true. We know that by faith. The Bible doesn't need defending.

  d. Yes, it is by what God has done in creation that we can know more of the awesome Lord we serve.

- **Class work.** Have the students read and answer the questions related to Romans 1:18–20; Genesis 1:20–25; and 1 Corinthians 15:39.

If you have additional time ...
Suggestions for augmenting lessons (home school, day school)

One or more extra sessions would be helpful. This class is also best integrated with life science or biology. The concepts of natural selection, mutations, genetic variation, heredity, etc., are detailed and can use some extra reinforcement.

Answers in Genesis has several resources available, including the book *Evolution Exposed: Biology* (chapter 3) and Ken Ham's talk 'Do Animals Evolve?' (a 30-minute video in the seminar series *Answers ... with Ken Ham*, available on DVD from www.AnswersInGenesis.org).

Blue eyes/Brown eyes cutouts

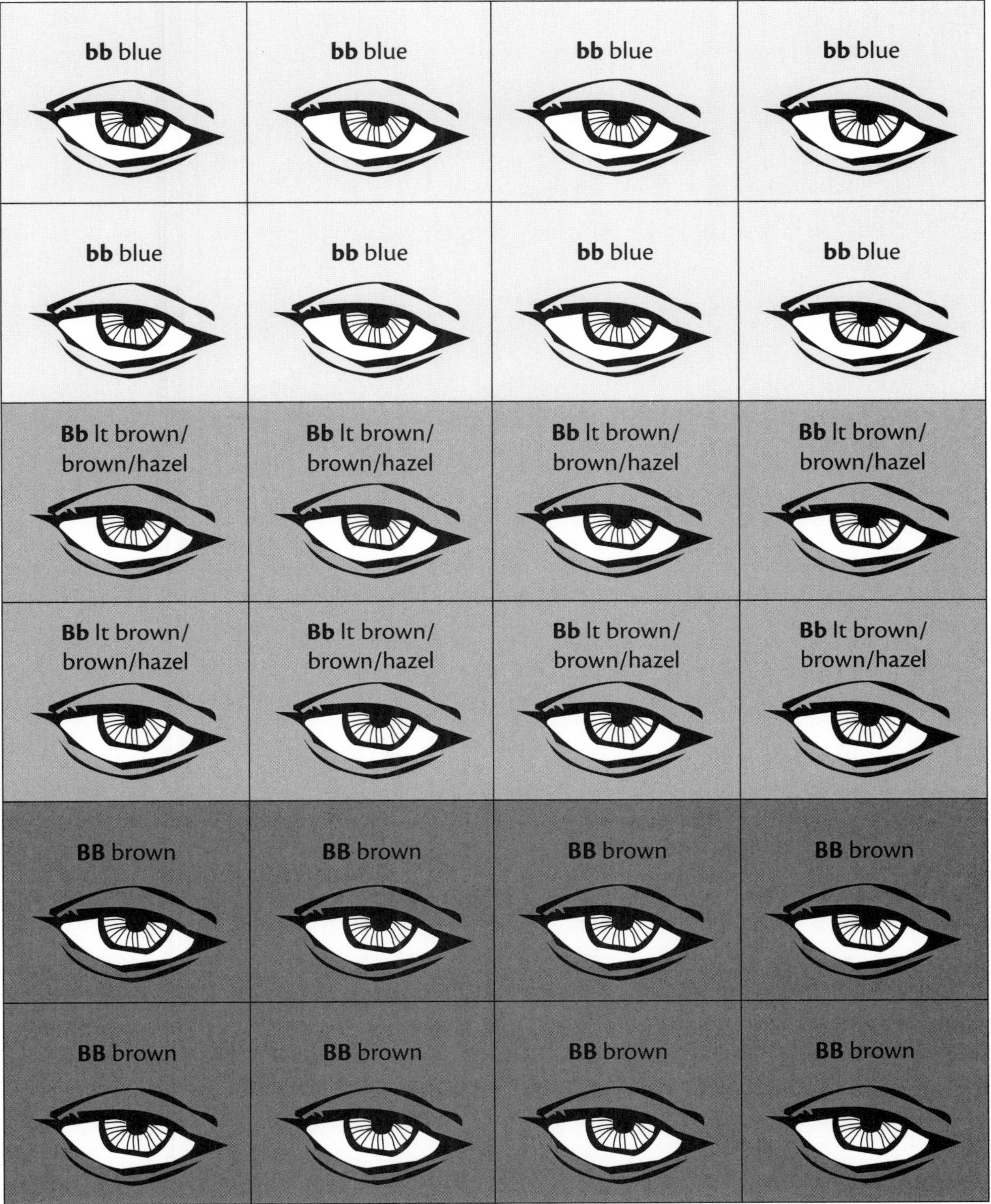

Please feel free to color in the eyes above.

Dog cutouts

small dog	small dog	small dog	small dog
small dog	small dog	small dog	small dog
medium dog	medium dog	medium dog	medium dog
medium dog	medium dog	medium dog	medium dog
large dog	large dog	large dog	large dog
large dog	large dog	large dog	large dog

Peppered moth cutouts

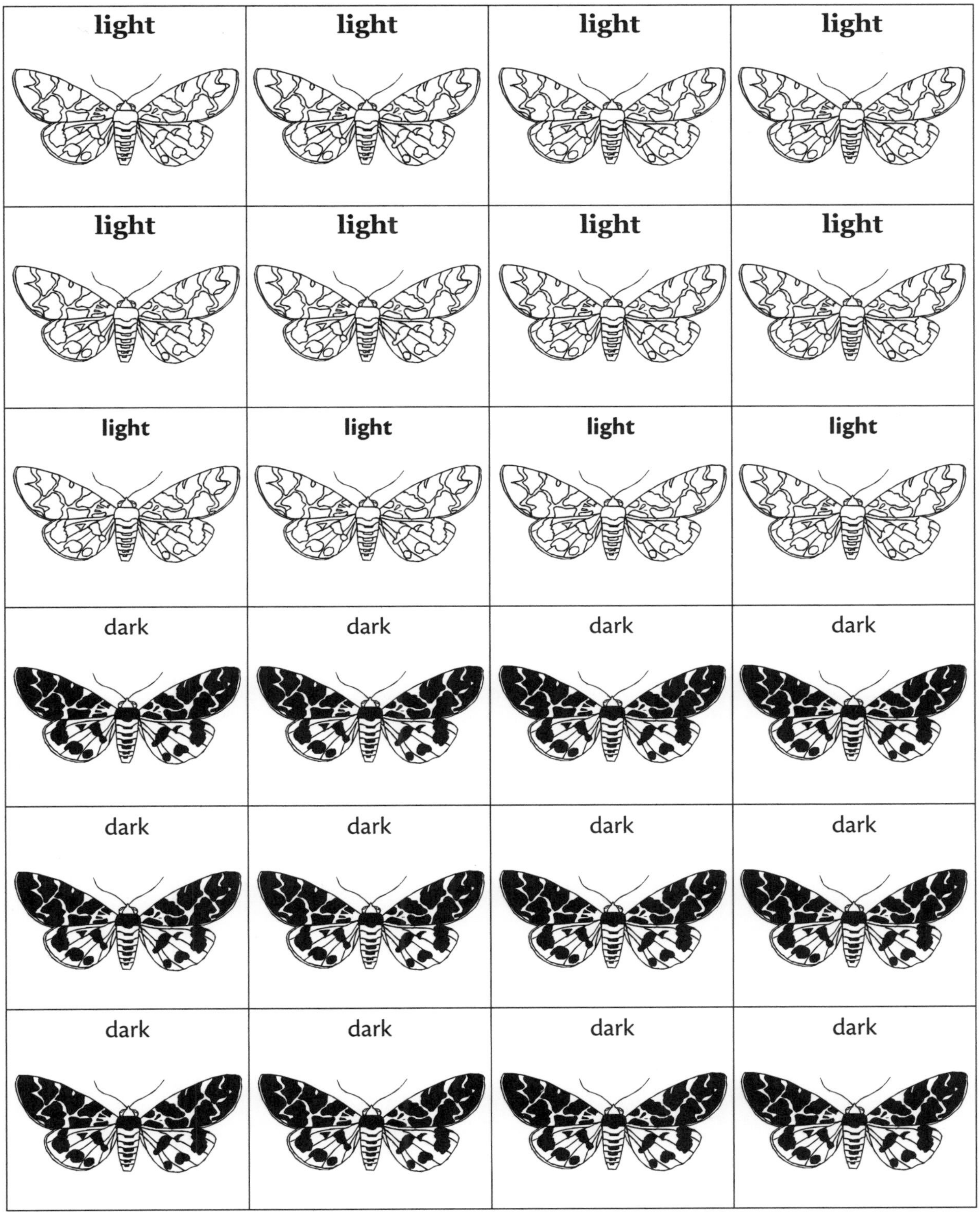

light	**light**	**light**	**light**
light	**light**	**light**	**light**
light	**light**	**light**	**light**
dark	dark	dark	dark
dark	dark	dark	dark
dark	dark	dark	dark

Mosquito cutouts

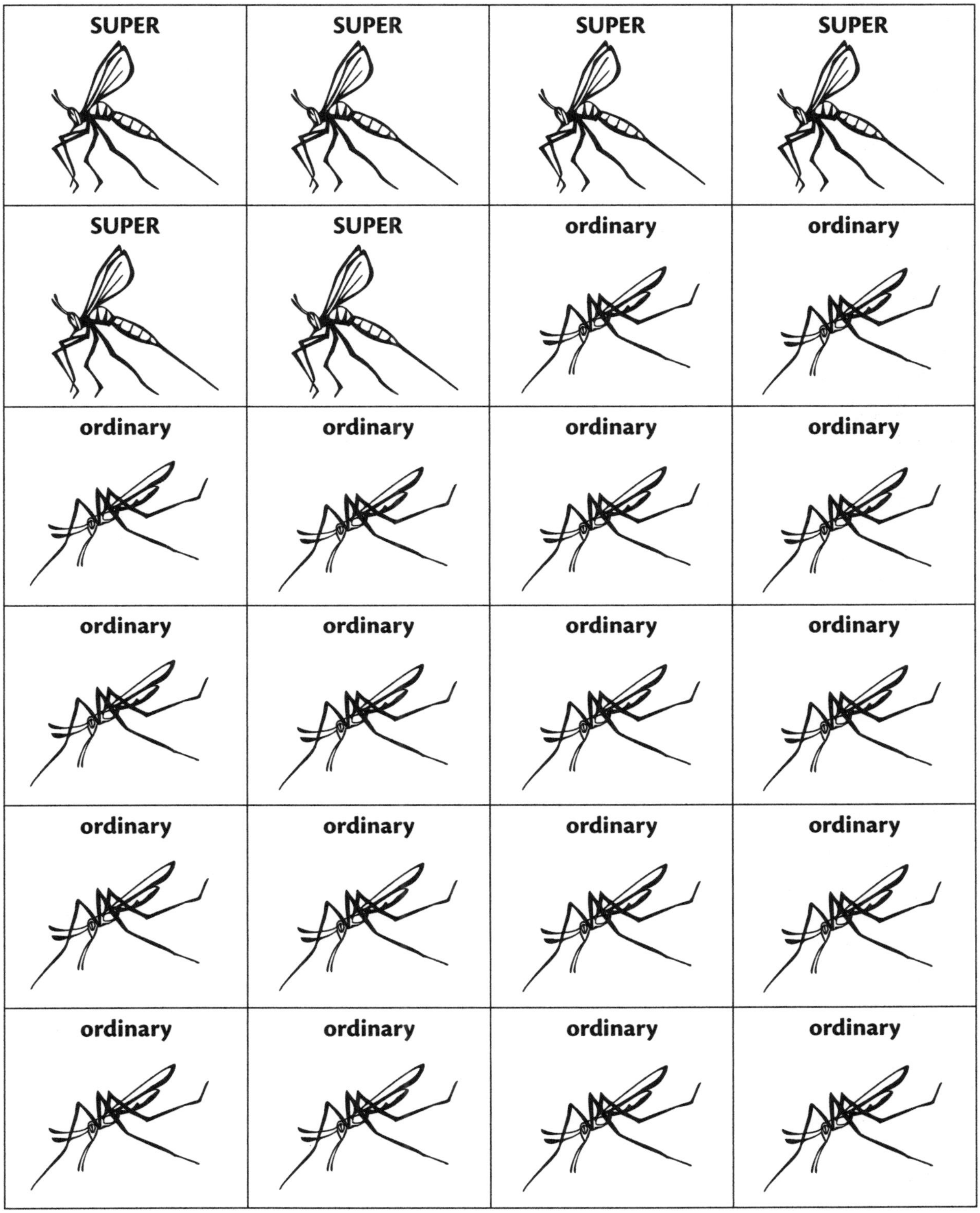

SUPER	SUPER	SUPER	SUPER
SUPER	SUPER	ordinary	ordinary
ordinary	ordinary	ordinary	ordinary
ordinary	ordinary	ordinary	ordinary
ordinary	ordinary	ordinary	ordinary
ordinary	ordinary	ordinary	ordinary

Melanin in skin cutouts

MM dark 	**MM** dark 	**MM** dark 	**MM** dark 
MM dark 	**MM** dark 	**MM** dark 	**MM** dark 
Mm medium 	**Mm** medium 	**Mm** medium 	**Mm** medium 
Mm medium 	**Mm** medium 	**Mm** medium 	**Mm** medium 
mm light 	**mm** light 	**mm** light 	**mm** light 
mm light 	**mm** light 	**mm** light 	**mm** light 

Sickle cell anemia cutouts

blood cell mutation: sickle cell 	blood cell mutation: sickle cell 	blood cell mutation: sickle cell 	blood cell mutation: sickle cell 
blood cell mutation: sickle cell 	normal red blood cell 	normal red blood cell 	normal red blood cell 
normal red blood cell 	normal red blood cell 	normal red blood cell 	normal red blood cell 
normal red blood cell 	normal red blood cell 	normal red blood cell 	normal red blood cell 
normal red blood cell 	normal red blood cell 	normal red blood cell 	normal red blood cell 
normal red blood cell 	normal red blood cell 	normal red blood cell 	normal red blood cell 

Beetles with and without wings cutouts

beetle with wings 	beetle with wings 	beetle with wings 	beetle with wings 
beetle with wings 	beetle with wings 	beetle with wings 	beetle with wings 
beetle with wings 	beetle with wings 	beetle with wings 	beetle with wings 
beetle without wings 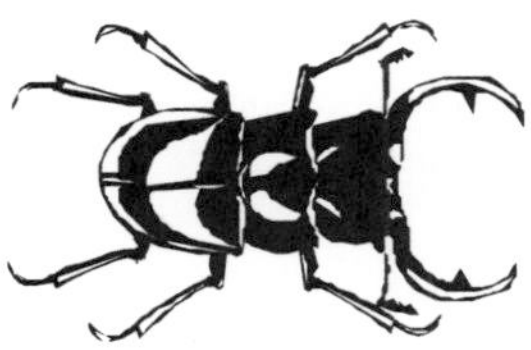	beetle without wings 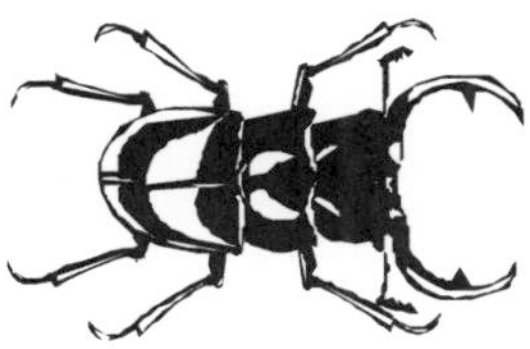	beetle without wings 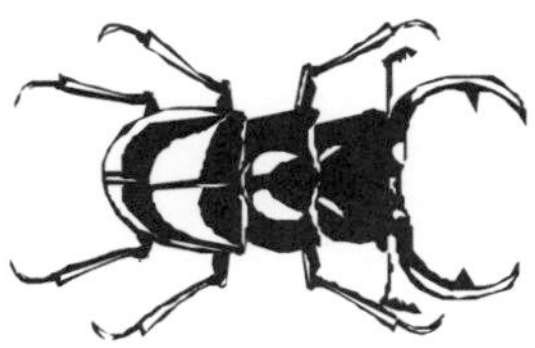	beetle without wings 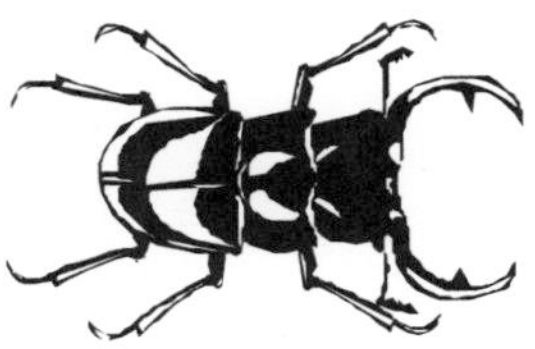
beetle without wings 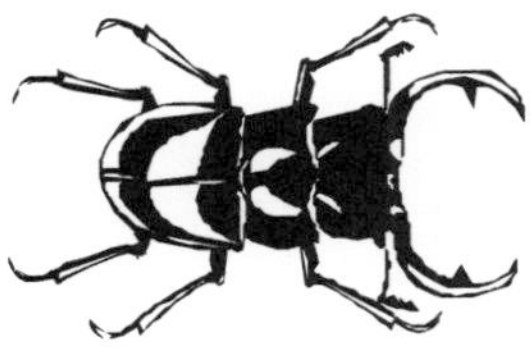	beetle without wings 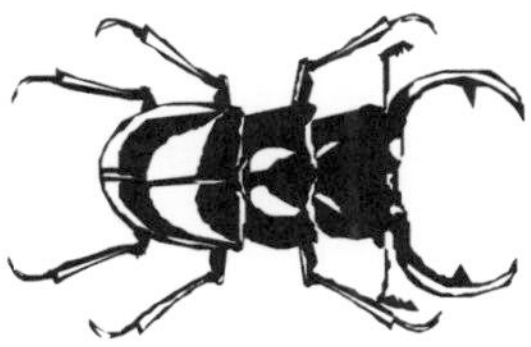	beetle without wings 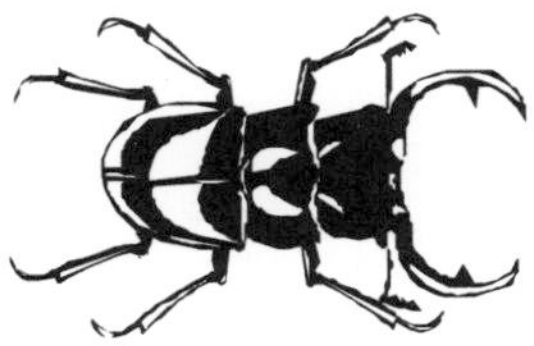	beetle without wings 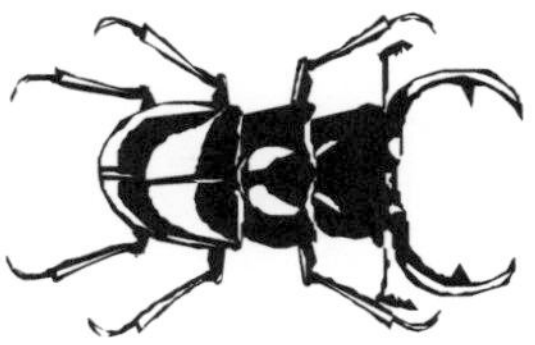
beetle without wings 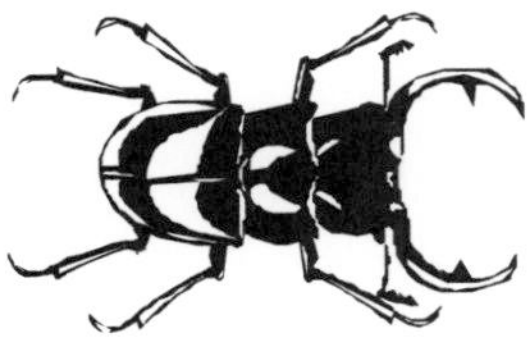	beetle without wings 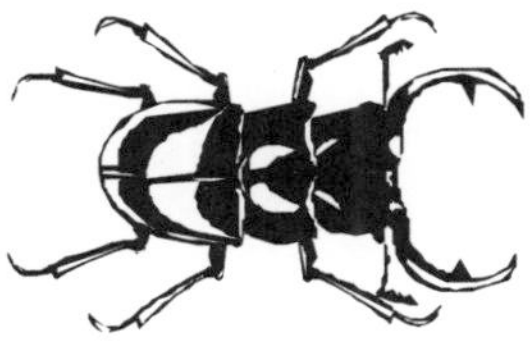	beetle without wings 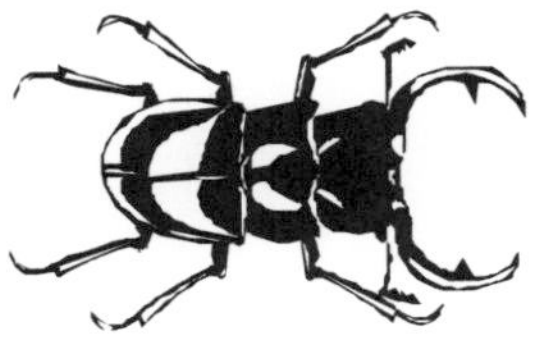	beetle without wings 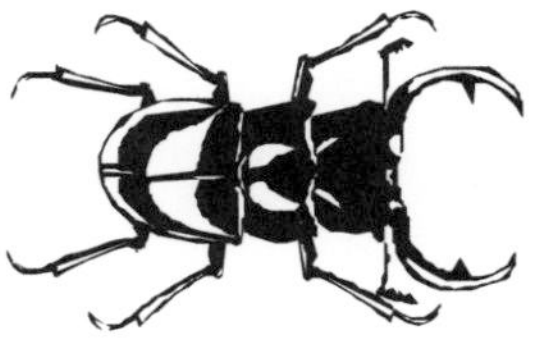

Fish with and without eyes cutouts

mutation—fish with no eyes 	mutation—fish with no eyes 	mutation—fish with no eyes 	mutation—fish with no eyes 
mutation—fish with no eyes 	mutation—fish with no eyes 	mutation—fish with no eyes 	mutation—fish with no eyes 
normal fish 	normal fish 	normal fish 	normal fish 
normal fish 	normal fish 	normal fish 	normal fish 
normal fish 	normal fish 	normal fish 	normal fish 
normal fish 	normal fish 	normal fish 	normal fish 

It All Begins With Genesis

LESSON 19

Recognizing different worldviews in science (part 5)

Origin of Mankind

Scripture: Genesis 1:26–27; 2:7, 21; Psalm 139:13; Job 33:4, 6

Suggested memory verse:

Job 33:4, 6

What this lesson is about:

Lessons 15–19 contrast the naturalistic and biblical worldviews in the scientific areas of the origin of the universe, rocks and fossils, life and groups of life, and mankind. Today's lesson focuses on the two major ways of looking at the origin of mankind. The challenging questions: Is it reasonable? Is it true? What does the eyewitness say? Which is compelling?

7 C's Connection: Creation, Corruption

Goals for the lesson: The student should

- be able to describe in a simple way the two worldviews concerning the origin of mankind.
- increase in his critical ability to think and evaluate both the presuppositions behind the two views and the message communicated by Scripture.
- begin to understand the importance of this issue as it relates to his whole worldview.

Preparation for lesson:

- Work through the student's lesson 19.
- Props needed: worldview eyeglasses, various illustrations from the curriculum CD, scramble-game pieces for review (from the previous lesson), assorted kitchenware
- Prepare five posters for a fossil lineup: australopithecines, *Homo habilis*, *Homo erectus*, Neanderthal, *Homo sapiens*. On the front of each poster attach the naturalistic explanation; on the back attach the biblical explanation. (Masters for this activity are found on the curriculum CD.)
- Signs to add to the bulletin board contrasting the two worldviews (illustrations 19-2, 19-3, 19-15)

19 Recognizing different worldviews in science (part 5)

Plan for lesson:

- **Review.** Since last week's lesson included a few new terms, it would be helpful to briefly review the concepts you introduced. You could use one of the scramble games that you didn't use in the last lesson. (Suggestion: peppered moths)

  1. Write the following on the board or on a transparency: genetic recombination, natural selection, mutation.
  2. Pass out the peppered moth pieces of paper. Tell them the story of the peppered moth example from history in England. Have them all stand up and then tell them that the trees are white and ask which moths would be easily seen and possibly eaten. (The black moths sit down.) Explain that this is as an example of both genetic recombination (different varieties of the same moth) and natural selection. Then tell them that the industrial revolution has come along and the trees are black. Ask who lives now. (White moths sit down.) In this illustration you can also teach mutations. What happens when a mutation causes one moth to have only one wing? Some people would call this evolution. Ask students what would make it evolution, as we have been using the term. (The moth would have to become something other than a moth.) It is important to help them see that genetic recombination, natural selection and mutations (because of the Fall) all occur in the biblical worldview. Most biology textbooks give examples of change *within kinds* in their evolution chapters, and then they extrapolate to evolution of new kinds. It is this extrapolation that does not fit into the biblical worldview.

- Introduce today's topic. (Use illustration 19-1—'People ... how did they all get here?') Using the naturalistic eyeglasses, ask students to explain how people could have gotten here apart from God. They should have no difficulty relating what they have seen in museums, textbooks, *National Geographic* and textbooks.

- Teach the naturalistic worldview. (Use illustration 19-2—'Origin of mankind: naturalism worldview.') At this point, take them briefly through the scenario from the first mammal to the 'common ancestor' and through the current hominid line.

  Teach the way presuppositions color and direct views about human 'evolution.'

  1. You might begin by showing an illustration or an actual article that announces a 'new find.'
  2. Illustrate how easy it is to place something (like bones) into an evolutionary order. You could arrange them in an imagined evolutionary order according to the size of their heads or the shape of their jaws or the color of their skin. Give them an assortment of kitchenware (various sizes of spoons, knives, forks and other more 'complex' implements) and ask them to arrange them in evolutionary order. Point out the 'wishful thinking' of those who are looking for 'missing links' and think they have found them.

3. Illustrate the manner in which artistic renditions can reveal the artist's presuppositions. (Use illustration 19-14—'The power of presuppositions.') Cover up the drawings and initially show the bones of the *Australopithecus boisei.* Ask if it would be possible to tell from the bones how much hair the creature possessed, the expression in the eyes, etc. Then show the three different renditions given for the same bones.

- **Activity.** Display the posters (masters included on the curriculum CD) for australopithecines, *Homo habilis, Homo erectus,* Neanderthal and *Homo sapiens,* and invite students to come forward and hold the posters in order to demonstrate the evolutionary sequence. (Leave illustration 19-2—the naturalistic position—on the screen.) Go through each poster and present the naturalistic view that is given on the poster. Ask: 'Is it reasonable? Is it true? Is there another way of looking at this data?'
- **Present biblical worldview.** (Use illustration 19-3—'Origin of mankind: biblical worldview.') Keep the children who are modeling the posters at the front of the room. Ask them to turn their posters over. Then go through each of the posters and give the creationist interpretation. Bottom line: man has always been man, with variations; apes have always been apes, with variations.
- **Sum it up.** (Use summary illustration 19-15—'Origin of mankind.') Compare the two worldviews. Ask, 'What does the eyewitness say?'
- **Class work.** Have the students work through the Scripture assignments given in their lesson and discuss them in small groups.

If you have additional time . . .
Suggestions for augmenting lessons (home school, day school)

One or more extra sessions would be helpful. This class can be integrated with a life science or biology class.

Dr Kurt Wise's lecture 6 "The Doctrine of Man" from the *Genesis Part 1* Precept course would effectively augment this study. Answers in Genesis has several other resources available, including the book *Evolution Exposed: Biology* (chapter 10), *The New Answers Book 2* (chapter 8), and the videos *Image of God or Planet of the Apes* and *Lucy: She's No Lady* (available from www.AnswersInGenesis.org).

Since this is the last in the series of worldviews, a Zonk session to review would be appropriate.

It All Begins With

Genesis

LESSON 20

How did evil come into the world?

Scripture: Genesis 3

Suggested memory verse:

Genesis 3:6

What this lesson is about:

This lesson serves as an overview of Genesis 3. The students will utilize their inductive Bible study skills in asking the Five W's and H questions and making observations regarding the content of Genesis 3.

7 C's Connection: Corruption

Goals for the lesson: The student should

- become more familiar with asking Five W's and H kinds of questions and with the technique of marking key words.
- be able to tell you the theme of Genesis 3 and the major people, places and events of the chapter.

Preparation for lesson:

- Work through the student's lesson 20.
- Prepare a game of Zonk as suggested at the end of this lesson. You will need index cards, markers, glue or tape, a list of questions, and prizes, if desired. Suggested questions are found in lesson 7.

Plan for lesson:

- **Review.** This lesson marks a transition from the past weeks, which focused on origins and worldviews, to a new segment on Genesis. You should spend a little time making the transition, helping the students to see once again the three-fold thrust of this course: learning inductive study, understanding worldviews and building a biblical worldview through the study of Genesis. You may want to review some of the facts and concepts you have taught over the past lessons by playing the game of Zonk. Allow at least 20 minutes for this activity (more, if time permits).
- **Class work.** Instruct students to take out the observation sheet for Genesis 3 and their colored markers. Instruct students to mark four key words: God, Adam, Eve and the serpent. Show them how to mark the words (on a transparency). Give them 10–15 minutes to complete the assignment.

- If time permits (it won't if you have only 40–50 minutes), assign other key words, as shown in the lesson: death, dying, curse. Or instruct students to work on answering the questions in the margin of the observation sheet. Or instruct them to draw a picture of events in chapter 3.
- **Discussion.** Work together to answer the major who, what, where and when questions answered by the chapter. Most are aware of the content of this chapter before they begin the assignment, so this discussion will serve merely to pull together their thoughts.

  Who? (God, Adam, Eve, serpent)

  Where? (Garden of Eden)

  When? (Sometime after man was created on Day 6. The text doesn't tell us.)

  What events? (Eve's temptation; Adam's and Eve's sin; Adam's and Eve's response to their sin; God's response to their sin and punishment; promise and hope (students probably won't see this); expulsion from the Garden)

  Why is this one of the most important chapters in Scripture? (It is pivotal. If this didn't happen, the rest of Scripture and the sacrifice of Christ wouldn't have been necessary. It explains sin, evil and all that is wrong in the world.)

If you have additional time . . .
Suggestions for augmenting lessons (home school, day school)

One extra session is recommended. This would allow a more leisurely and detailed observation of Genesis 3. You will also need time to review the inductive study principles introduced during the first part of the course. This is a good time for a Zonk review (instructions and sample questions in lesson 7).

Ken Ham has a helpful talk on 'Why Is There Death and Suffering?' (in the *Answers ... with Ken Ham* series, available on DVD from www.AnswersInGenesis.org). See also chapter 26 of *The New Answers Book 1*.

It All Begins With
Genesis
LESSON
21
Temptation and sin

Scripture:

Genesis 3; Isaiah 53:6; Romans 14:23; James 4:17; 1 John 3:4; 2:16; James 1:13–15; Hebrews 4:14–16; Matthew 26:41; 6:9; 1 Corinthians 10:12; Psalm 119:11; Philippians 4:8; 2 Timothy 2:22; 2 Corinthians 10:3; Galatians 5:16

Suggested memory verse:

Philippians 4:8

What this lesson is about:

The focus of this lesson is the subject of temptation. It begins with a dramatization and discussion of Eve's temptation in the Garden. It includes the definition of temptation and sin, the forms temptation takes and the progression from temptation to sin. The lesson further addresses the question of how a Christian can deal with temptation.

7 C's Connection: Corruption

Goals for the lesson: The student should

- be able to discuss the serpent's temptation and Eve's response.
- be able to define temptation and sin and know when a temptation becomes a sin.
- be able to identify the three types of temptations Eve faced and the form they take today.
- recognize from cross-references some biblical principles that help the Christian resist temptation.

Preparation for lesson:

- Work through the student's lesson 21.
- Prepare transparencies or posters that illustrate the definitions of temptation and sin and the three types of temptations Eve faced. (Examples are found on the CD.)
- Other suggested props, if available:

  'Apple' for Eve's temptation
  Hershey kisses or other appropriate 'temptations' for the class
  Tube of toothpaste; dart board
  Fishing rod and lure

Plan for lesson:

- **Introduction.** When the students are seated, distribute some Hershey 'kisses' or other attractive candy at each table. Give the class specific instructions: they are not to touch or eat the candy that is in front of them, on penalty of certain punishment.
- Direct their attention to the first question on the first page of their lesson for today. Ask your the students what 1 John 3:8 teaches about the reason Jesus came. You then would say that our purpose this lesson is to learn more about temptation and sin and how the devil works.
- **Drama.** It is interesting and helpful to dramatize the biblical story of the temptation. Appoint someone to play the part of the serpent and someone to play the part of the woman, and after each exchange ask the class the questions provided for you. Be sure that they see the tactics of the serpent, the responses of the woman and when the temptation actually becomes sin.
- **Teach** the difference between temptation and sin. Use transparencies or signs to illustrate the meaning of the Hebrew words (illustrations 21-1 and 21-2 on the CD). When you teach the meaning of *nasah* (temptation), you could illustrate by squeezing a tube of toothpaste. The illustration for *chata* (sin) will be remembered more easily if you can obtain a dartboard and show how one can 'miss the mark.'
- **Class work and discussion.** Have the students go through the biblical definitions of sin as found in the Isaiah, Romans, James and 1 John cross-references. If your time is limited, do the work with them and discuss as you go.
- Direct the group to 1 John 2:16 and ask them to find the three different temptations. It would then be helpful to use illustration 21-3 or write the three on the board. These apply to Eve's temptation and to the common temptations around us today. You can assign portions of this for independent work, or you can discuss as you go. Invite them to share some of the temptations that are most difficult for them.
- **Teach** next the progression from temptation to sin. Direct the class to James 1:13–15. Let them work on this independently and then discuss, or if time is short, do the work together. You can use the illustration of a fish and how he is tempted. (Use a fishing rod with bait and invite a student to be the fish.) First, you see the fish swimming around, minding its own business; next he is attracted to the lure. Then he swims back and forth gazing at it, perhaps touching it (you can prolong this process of being tempted). Finally, he grabs the bait, and the 'sin' has happened. You can ask how this fish could have avoided the temptation (by swimming away from the bait, by staying in the 'shelter of the rock,' etc.)
- **Class work.** The final, important part of the lesson involves searching through cross-references for the principles a Christian needs to learn to deal with temptation. Give them time to work on this alone, to highlight the principle they find in each verse.
- **Discussion.** After they have finished, ask students to give you the principles they learned and list them on the board. If time permits, there is much material for discussion and practical application. Emphasize the principle of 'Philippians 4:8–ing' their thoughts.

If you have additional time ...
(home school, day school) Suggestions for augmenting lessons.

One extra session would be helpful in order to allow a more leisurely trip through the cross-references and more time to apply the lesson to life. This is a good lesson to reinforce the observation/interpretation/application progression of inductive study.

It All Begins With Genesis

LESSON 22

Portrait of the serpent

Scripture: Genesis 3; Revelation 20:1–3; 12:7–9; John 8:44; Hebrews 2:14–15; 1 John 5:19; 2 Corinthians 2:10–11; 4:3–4; 11:14–15; Ephesians 2:1–2; 1 Peter 5:8; 2 Timothy 2:26

Suggested memory verse:

Genesis 3:1a

What this lesson is about:

This lesson introduces a new Bible study tool: the character study. The students will learn about the tempter by studying cross-references from Scripture, answering the Five W's and H kinds of questions, and then classifying the information into a word portrait of the tempter.

7 C's Connection: Corruption

Goals for the lesson: The student should

- learn more about the character and tactics of the evil one.
- learn how a biblical character study is done.
- improve in his ability to observe text and answer the Five W's and H questions in a precise way.

Preparation for lesson:

- Work through the student's lesson 22.
- Props needed:

  A large sheet of poster board paper, cut into the shape of 'devil'

  Smaller signs labeled *What is he called? What is he like? What does he do?* to be attached to the larger poster

  3x5 index cards, each with one of the Scripture references written on it. These will be applied to the Satan poster as the students go through the cross-references.

  A sign labeled *Topical study* (illustration 22-1 on the curriculum CD) with a list of steps in doing topical study … to be posted on the inductive study bulletin board

  Concordance and/or computer printout of results of a search for the words 'devil,' 'Satan,' 'dragon' and 'evil one'

Plan for lesson:

- **Review** principles you feel you need to stress from last week's lesson on temptation. Tell the students that last week you studied sin and temptation, and this week you are going to look at the one who does the tempting.
- **Introduce topical study.** Point out something else you learn to do when you learn inductive study (topical study). Begin by asking: ' If you are someone who wants to have a biblical worldview, you need to know what the Bible says about different things in life, don't you? For example, you need to know what the Bible says about drinking, about marriage, about pornography, about lying—about anything on how to live. How do you find out these things? By doing a *topical study.* (Show a sign or illustration that explains topical study. You can use illustration 22-1 on the curriculum CD.) You would look up in the Bible the word(s) you are interested in, read everything Scripture says and then see what questions are answered. Then you pull it together in a meaningful way: in a chart, in a list or in a story.
- Explain that today we are going to do a topical study on the serpent, first mentioned in Genesis 3. You could spend a little time talking about why this would be helpful to know. You can introduce the study of the serpent by talking about all the caricatures of the devil: the man in red pajamas with a pitchfork, etc. Obviously, these caricatures minimize who he really is. You can also ask them if they have heard people deny the existence of the devil. Some Christians accept the existence of God but deny the devil.
- **Work together on the beginning steps of this study.** Instruct students to take out the chart 'Portrait of the serpent' from their lesson. They will be adding to it throughout the lesson. They will also need their observation sheet for Genesis 3.

    1. Illustrate the many mentions of Satan, 'evil one,' and other expressions for him in Scripture by showing them a printout taken from a computer search, or by showing them a concordance. Tell them you will be looking at only a fraction of the verses listed.
    2. Go through the chapter noting the markings made of 'serpent' in a previous lesson. Talk students through the questions that are answered by the text. For example:

        First 'pitchfork' verse: verse 1. What are we told about the serpent? *(He was more crafty than any beast of the field. That tells us something about what the serpent is like, doesn't it? So we will mark that and transfer it to our chart on the serpent.)* Point out that this note has already been written on their chart, as an example for them. You may then take an index card with 'crafty (Gen. 3:1)' written on it and attach it to the Satan poster.

        Next mention verse 4. What is the serpent doing here? *(He lied to her. He denied God's Word. That tells us more about what he is like, doesn't it?)* Instruct them to write 'liar, denies God's Word' on their sheets, and attach the pre-written verse card to the poster.

        Go next to verse 13. What did the serpent do? *(He deceived. That tells us something about what the serpent does.)* Instruct them to write 'deceives' under 'What does he do?' on their chart. Then attach a card to the poster.

Mark together the fill-in questions about verses 14–15. Don't go into any detail about them other than to say that this is the first time in the Bible that the Gospel is foretold. We'll study that in a later lesson.

- **Class work.** There are 13 cross-references printed in their lesson. Each will answer one or more of the questions 'What is he called?' 'What is he like?' 'What does he do?' Assign the verses to the students and instruct them to transfer what they learn over to their charts. How you do this will depend on the time available to you and the maturity of your group. They may be able to complete the assignment on their own, with you available to answer questions as they arise, or you may wish to divide the group and assign different verses to different students. You may wish to do some of the verses together.
- **Discussion**. After students have finished their work, go through a completed chart on the board, so they can check their answers. When you hear their answers, you can then attach the appropriate verse cards to the serpent poster. If you see they will not be able to get through all the verses, be sure to stop them in time to help them complete the chart.

  Ask, 'What have you learned about the serpent that you didn't know before?'

If you have additional time ...
Suggestions for augmenting lessons (home school, day school)

One extra session would be helpful for this lesson. It would allow a more leisurely study of the cross-references, with a more detailed discussion of the tempter and how to do a topical study.

It All Begins With Genesis

LESSON 23

The fallen world

Scripture: Genesis 3; Romans 8:20–22; Ephesians 2:1–3

Suggested memory verse:

Ephesians 2:1

What this lesson is about:

This lesson presents the broader picture of the widespread effects of the Fall of mankind. It includes closer observation of Genesis 3:7–13 and an examination of sin's impact on relationships, on activities and on the earth itself.

7 C's Connection: Corruption

Goals for the lesson: The student should

- understand what happened as a result of man's sin—the widespread effects of sin on people's relationships to one another and to God.
- consider the changes to the created order brought about by man's sin.

Preparation for lesson:

- Work through the student's lesson 23.
- Prepare a large poster titled 'When sin came into the world ....' You might place a big black border around it. You will complete the poster while you teach. You will also need a black marker.
- Collect recent newspapers. You will need scissors and glue, tape or staples.
- You may wish to dress in black.

Plan for lesson:

- **Introduction.** Dress in black and ask students if they know why you dressed that way for today's lesson. Tell them the purpose of this lesson is to help them picture total separation from God, the result of the Fall. We know that God provided a way back to Him, but for today we're going to imagine what a cursed world is all about.
- **Class work.** Instruct the students to have both lesson 23 and the Genesis 3 worksheet beside them. Ask them to complete the first three and one-half pages of the lesson (all the questions *before* the paragraph that begins 'You will find a chart located at the end of this lesson ...').

- **Discussion.** While the students are working, place the large sign 'When sin came into the world ...' in front of the group. As you discuss each question and hear their answers, write the results of the Fall on the poster. Instruct them to write the same answers on their chart, located at the end of their lesson.

  Examples of answers to write on the sign:

  > Shame, fear/hiding, blame-shifting, pain (in childbirth), relationship problems between husband and wife, other relationship problems, ground cursed with thorns and thistles, difficulty of work with sweat and toil, death.

- **Class work and discussion.** Now we will look at something said in the New Testament that tells us more about what happened in Genesis 3. Instruct the students to circle every mention of creation (or its pronoun) in **Romans 8:20–22.**

  Answer together the Five W's and H questions given.

  > Verse 20: The creation was *subjected to frustration.*
  >
  > Verse 20: The creation did not subject itself, but it was done *by God's will.*
  >
  > Verse 21: God subjected the creation to frustration in hope that it would be freed from its bondage to *decay.*
  >
  > Verse 22: The creation is *groaning.*
  >
  > This groaning and decay must have begun after the Fall.
  >
  > The groaning and decay will end after Jesus returns and a new heaven and earth is established.
  >
  > Examples of groaning and decay: earthquakes, volcanoes, fire, drought, hurricanes, diseases, floods, etc.

  Write on the big chart 'decay,' 'groaning creation' and other examples, while your students write them on their own charts.

- **Class work and discussion.** Refer the students to the **Ephesians 2:1–3** passage. We saw that death (spiritual as well as physical) came to man after the Fall. This passage tells us more about what a spiritually dead person is like. Instruct the students to circle all the personal pronouns in the passage. Then ask them the Five W's and H questions given. Transfer the answers to the big chart and instruct them to write them on their sin chart as well.

  > Verse 1: The person who does not have Christ is *dead.*
  >
  > Verse 2: These dead persons followed *the ways of this world, the ruler of the kingdom of the air* (this spirit is Satan).
  >
  > Verse 2: These persons are described as *disobedient.*

Verse 3: These persons *gratify the cravings of their flesh* and *follow the flesh's desires and thoughts.* (Ask for examples of this.)

Verse 3: These dead people are described as *objects of wrath.*

- **Activity.** Distribute recent newspapers to the class, along with scissors. Instruct students to cut out headlines that illustrate the effects of the Fall. This is an extremely effective way to help them see the pervasiveness of the effects of sin in our world. You can post the headlines on the ongoing time line under the Fall, or if your poster is large enough, they could be pasted on the poster.
- **Conclusion.** Discuss the worldview questions 'Where does evil come from?' 'How could a good God allow such bad things to happen?' Students should easily see that man is responsible for the bad things that happen. God gave him the choice, and man's sin brought this death, decay and corruption into the world.

If you have additional time ...
Suggestions for augmenting lessons (home school, day school)

One extra session is recommended. This would allow for a more thorough discussion of the cross-references and a better pulling together of all the principles. The newspaper search is an exercise the students will enjoy, and the extra time would allow for that activity.

It All Begins With

Genesis

LESSON 24

God's solution

Scripture: Genesis 3; Leviticus 17:11; Luke 19:10

Suggested memory verse:

Genesis 3:15

What this lesson is about:

This is our last lesson on Genesis 3. God's solution to the Fall is seen in this lesson, as we look at three aspects of His grace illustrated in the chapter. This lesson also provides a return to the focus on developing a biblical worldview, as we look at what a biblical worldview would explain about 'who is man' and 'what is the origin of death and suffering.'

7 C's Connection: Corruption, Christ, Cross, Consummation

Goals for the lesson: The student should

- be able to tell you three ways God's grace is shown in Genesis 3.
- be able to answer the following questions from both a biblical worldview and a naturalistic worldview: 'Who is man?' 'How can death and suffering in the world be explained?'
- demonstrate an understanding of temptation, sin, the serpent and the other facts of Genesis 3 during a review of the chapter.

Preparation for lesson:

- Work through the student's lesson 24.
- Prepare illustration of Genesis 3:15.
- Prepare Zonk questions for Genesis 3. Prizes for the winning team are always appreciated.
- Props: worldview 'eyeglasses'

Plan for lesson:

- **Review.** Since you probably were not able to devote enough time to the results of the Fall in last week's lesson, a good way to review would be (1) to have the students draw pictures of the world of the Fall or (2) to have them paint word pictures of the extent of the Fall. You could perhaps arrive in class dressed in black and wearing a dejected countenance. You could tell them that you are Adam (or Eve) and you have sinned and God has pronounced the Curse, and you are realizing all that comes with the punishment. Have students tell you all that has changed because of their sin.

- Then you can divide your visual aid (white board or poster board) into three parts, and tell the students that we will see three ways God deals with the problem in Genesis 3. Title the visual aid 'God's solution.'

- **Dramatization of solution 1.** Write Genesis 3:15 on the board or use an overhead. Students are capable of working through this on their own, but it is not easy for some to grasp, so it would probably be better to walk them through part of it. Tell them this is the 'protoevangelium,' the first proclamation of the Gospel. Then go through it with them (using the word studies and writing the definitions of 'enmity,' 'seed' and 'bruise' above the verse on the board.)

  It may be helpful to dramatize the verse by calling up one student to represent the woman and another to represent the seed. Then portray 'enmity' between them. Next call two students to represent the seed of the woman and the seed of the serpent. Demonstrate continued enmity. Then demonstrate (lightly, of course!) the seed of the serpent bruising the heel of the seed of the woman, and the seed of the woman bruising the head of the seed of the serpent. Ask which is the fatal wound?

- **Class work.** After you have discussed the meaning of the verse, give them time either to draw a picture of the verse or to re-write the verse in their own words (or you can ask them to do both).

- **Discuss solution 2.** God makes clothes for Adam and Eve.

- **Class work.** Have them answer the questions in this section. Follow the class work by discussion to be sure they understand this to be the first shedding of blood, a blood sacrifice provided by God Himself in order to cover the sin of Adam and Eve. You may have the opportunity to ask the students why we wear clothing today, even if it is hot. It all goes back to the Fall.

- **Discuss solution 3.** God sends the man and woman from the Garden so they will not eat of the Tree of Life and live forever. This is something they can do in class if time allows.

- **Discuss worldviews.** Use your two different kinds of eyeglasses and remind the students that one of the purposes of our study this year is to help them find good biblical answers to important worldview questions, and to be able to see how someone who doesn't wear biblical eyeglasses would come up with very different, unsatisfying answers.

  Put on the naturalistic eyeglasses, and remind them that this person doesn't believe in the Bible, in God or in any such thing as a Fall. This person doesn't even believe that there is any such thing as sin.

  How would they answer the question 'Who is man?' *(He is an accident, up from the slime, with no purpose, no future, nobody to be accountable to.)*

  'What is the reason for death, sorrow and suffering?' *(evolutionary struggle for survival, no purpose in the universe, hopelessness)*

'How would you 'fix' it?' *(new government programs, money, blaming others, hopelessness)*

Then put on the biblical eyeglasses. You could ask, 'From what you have learned about man's creation and Fall, what can you say about who man is?' *(He is created in the image of God, so he is special and capable of greatness. He is also fallen and is capable of much wretchedness. Both exist in man. But he also has a purpose and a future, because God loved him and chose to die for him.)*

'What is the reason for death, sorrow and suffering? How would you 'fix' it?' *(Man's sin caused the entire creation to be cursed. We live with the results of man's sin today. But we also have God's promise that the creation will be restored and man can be saved, so we have hope in the midst of the suffering. Preach the Gospel, minister to the suffering, have hope knowing God is in control and a new heavens and earth have been promised.)*

- **Review. Play Zonk.** This would be a good opportunity for a review of all the lessons on Genesis 3. Allow about 30 minutes, if possible. Sample questions follow (and you can also make your own questions). See directions in lesson 7.

If you have additional time . . .
Suggestions for augmenting lessons (home school, day school)

One extra session is recommended. You could use it to reinforce the concepts that still seem 'fuzzy' and to play a Zonk game to review chapter 3.

Zonk questions: Review of Genesis 3

100-point questions	**What kind of animal tempts Eve in the Garden?** **What is God's curse on the serpent?** *(go on your belly—head ultimately crushed)* **What is God's curse on the woman?** *(pain in childbirth, desire for husband and he will rule over her)* **What is God's curse on the man?** *(toil in work, ultimate death)* **What kind of clothing did Adam and Eve put on after they sinned?** *(fig leaves)* **What kind of clothing did God provide for Adam and Eve?** *(animal skins)*
200-point questions	**At what point did Eve's temptation turn into a sin?** *(when she ate)* **The Hebrew word '*nasah*' means an attempt to prove the quality of something, to put to the test. What's another definition of *nasah*?** *(temptation)* **The Hebrew word '*chata*' means 'missing the mark.' What is another word to define *chata*?** *(sin)* **Whom did Adam blame for his having eaten the fruit (two answers)?** *(God and Eve)* **Was the creation itself cursed? How?** *(thorns and thistles, groaning, decay)*
300-point questions	**Name three other names that mean the same thing as the 'serpent.'** **Where in the Garden was the forbidden tree found?** *(middle of the Garden, verse 3)* **When Eve saw that the fruit was good to eat, what kind of temptation was she experiencing?** *(lust of the flesh)* **When did the first animal sacrifice occur?** *(when God provided clothing for Adam and Eve)* **When Eve saw that the fruit was pleasing to the eye, which of the three kinds of temptation was she experiencing?** *(lust of the eyes)* **When Eve heard that eating the fruit would make her like God, knowing good and evil, which of the three temptations was that appealing to?** *(pride of life, boasting of what a person has and does)* **One way we are tempted is by the cravings of sinful man (lust of the flesh). Give two illustrations of this temptation in our lives today.** **Another way we are tempted is by the lust of the eyes. Give two illustrations of this temptation in our lives today.** **Another way we are tempted is by boasting of what we have and do (pride of life). Give two illustrations of this temptation in our lives today.**

400-point questions

When the serpent says to Eve during the temptation, 'Indeed, has God said, "You shall not eat from any tree of the garden," ' what is the serpent doing? *(questioning God's Word, distorting God's Word, adding to God's Word)*

In order to avoid temptation, you should 'frisk' the dirty thought and 'Philippians 4:8 it.' What does that mean?

Who named Eve? What does Eve mean? *(Adam—because she was mother of all the living, verse 20)*

What two emotions did Adam and Eve experience right after they sinned? *(shame and fear)*

In 1 Peter 5:8 the devil, our enemy, is said to prowl around like what? *(a roaring lion looking for someone to devour)*

In 2 Corinthians 11:14 we are told that the devil often masquerades as what? *(an angel of light)*

In John 8:44, Jesus tells us that the devil is a murderer and also he is 'the father of _______.' *(lies)*

When God spoke about the seed of the woman in Genesis 3:15, to whom was He referring?

What did God mean when He said the seed of the serpent would bruise the seed of the woman on the heel? *(Christ's crucifixion)*

What did God mean when He said the seed of the woman would bruise the seed of the serpent on the head? *(Christ would give a fatal blow to Satan.)*

500-point questions

Name three ways that God showed mercy to fallen man in Genesis 3.

Temptation comes in three different forms. Name them.

James 1:13 tells us the progression from temptation to sin. Fill in the blanks: Each person is tempted when, by his own evil desire, he is dragged away and enticed. Then after desire has conceived, it gives birth to _______; and _______ when it is full grown, gives birth to __________. *(sin, sin, death)*

How does Scripture tell us we can avoid temptation? *(possible answers: watch and pray, draw near to Jesus, ask the Father not to lead us into temptation, 'Philippians 4:8 it,' memorize the Word, flee youthful lusts, walk in the Spirit)*

Why did God cast Adam and Eve out of the Garden? How did that show mercy to Adam and Eve?

Where did Adam and Eve go after they were sent from the Garden? *(east of Eden)*

What kept Adam and Eve from going back into the Garden again? *(cherubim and a flaming sword, which turned every direction to guard the way to the Tree of Life, verse 24)*

What is the protoevangelium? *(Genesis 3:15—the first mention of the Good News to come)*

How would someone with a biblical worldview explain the reason there is suffering and pain and death in the world today?

How would someone with a naturalistic worldview explain the reason for suffering, sin and death in the world?

It All Begins With Genesis — LESSON 25

Life in the fallen world: Cain and Abel

Scripture: Genesis 4:1–16; Hebrews 9:22; 11:4

Suggested memory verse (choose one):

Genesis 4:16; Hebrews 9:22b

What this lesson is about:

This lesson begins to look at life as lived out under the Curse. Its focus is Genesis 4:1–16 and the story of Cain and Abel. The question to be addressed: 'How does one come to God: His way or ours?'

7 C's Connection: Corruption

Goals for the lesson: The student should

- understand that there are basically two choices in life: do things our way, or do things God's way. Cain chose to do things his way; Abel chose God's way.
- understand that God has made His way clear from the beginning through His Word.
- know why God accepted Abel's offering but rejected Cain's offering.
- see more of the character of God in His dealings with Cain.

Preparation for lesson:

- Work through the student's lesson 25.
- Prepare props: one platter with a hunk of raw red meat and another with some beautiful fruit or vegetables.

Plan for lesson:

- **Introduction.** Explain that now we will begin a series of chapters that will help us to see what happened in a world that was cursed by sin. Ask students to take out their observation worksheets for Genesis 4.
- **Class work.** Give students about 10 minutes to read through the first 16 verses and mark 'Cain,' 'Abel,' 'God' and 'offering.' It would probably be helpful to suggest how to mark each word by drawing them on white board or a transparency. You will not have time to allow them to tarry on this assignment.
- **Teaching.** Ask students if they know that there are two choices for what to do in life: our way or God's way (as expressed on the first page of today's student lesson). Ask how we know which is

His way (His Word). Use the situations given and ask how they would know which pleases God. Work through this section together.

- **Class work and discussion.** Give them about 5 minutes to complete the questions under the section 'Cain and Abel come to God,' beginning on the second page of today's lesson. Briefly go through the answers with them.
- **Illustration.** Have two platters in front of the class. On one have bloody, uncooked meat. On the other have an attractive arrangement of fruit or vegetables. Ask, 'Which is pleasing to God and why?' They have two cross-references from Hebrews that explain why Cain's offering was rejected and Abel's was accepted. Let this be class work, if you have time.
- **Role-play.** What happened after Cain murdered his brother and God confronted him? This is another good scene to dramatize (p. 149 in the student workbook). Ask someone to play Cain and someone to play God. (Abel also has a very short part.) After each exchange, pose the questions for discussion and let the class answer them as you go. Be sure to help them see the similarities between the way God approached Cain after his sin and Adam after his. Ask, 'Why is Cain's punishment so bad? God hasn't killed him, and He has protected him?' (Help them to see how separation from God is the worst punishment of all.)
- **Sum it up.** How do we know how we should approach God? What happens when we do it our way, not His? Perhaps you could share an example from your own life to illustrate this, and then ask for their examples.

  (If you have any extra time in this class, it would be helpful to go back to the observation sheet and let students identify the 'firsts' in the chapter, choose the theme of the chapter and draw a picture of the main events of the chapter.)

If you have additional time . . .
Suggestions for augmenting lessons (home school, day school)

One extra session is recommended. This is the first study of chapter 4, and it would be helpful to take time to go through the observation sheet and answer the questions in the margin *before* you get into detail on Cain and Abel.

It All Begins With

Genesis

LESSON 26

Life in the fallen world: Adam's descendants

Scripture: Genesis 4:17–25; 5:1–32

Suggested memory verse:

Genesis 5:5

What this lesson is about:

This lesson covers Genesis 4–5. It basically illustrates life under the Curse being played out: '. . . and he died.' It also shows two family trees. The first indicates the line of Cain—those who went out from the presence of the Lord. The second line were those who began 'to call upon the name of the LORD.' In this lesson we see the development of civilization in the years following the Fall. This development, as reported in Scripture, is vastly different from what is generally reported in secular history books.

7 C's Connection: Corruption

Goals for the lesson: The student should

- understand that two lines diverged after the Fall. One descended from Cain and was made up of those who 'went out from the presence of the LORD.' The other was made up of those who 'called upon the name of the LORD.'
- see the effects of the Curse in the statement 'and he died.'
- be able to identify Enoch and who he is in biblical history.
- recognize the relatively advanced civilization developed by pre-Flood man.

Preparation for lesson:

- Work through the student's lesson 26.
- Prepare activity for the two lines of descent. (Place this activity under the 'Fall' section of your time-line bulletin board, if you have one. If you don't have space for that, use two sheets of poster board, one labeled in blue 'The line of Cain' and the other labeled in red 'The line of Seth.')

  Draw a vertical line on each board. The various names will be attached to this line at the appropriate times during the lesson presentation.

  Prepare strips of paper (or index cards) that include a descendant's name on each. Use blue ink for Cain's family and red ink for Seth's family.

  Also prepare some pictures (you can use clip art from your computer) that will illustrate the development of civilization. You should have pictures to depict an ancient city, tent dwellers and shepherds, musical lyre and pipe, metallurgy and violence. Each picture will be placed on the poster board family line at the appropriate time during the lesson.

Finally, prepare some strips of paper with 'and he died at . . . [include the age].' Be sure to include one for Enoch, who didn't die. These will also be attached to the poster at the appropriate time in the lesson.

When you finish the activity, you will have a visual aid for the line of Cain and the line of Seth. This should be helpful as you go on to discuss the Flood and later the genealogies of Shem, Ham and Japheth, at which time you will use the same kind of illustration.

Plan for lesson:

- **Review** anything needed to reinforce last week's teaching about Cain and Abel. You could ask again why God did not accept Cain's sacrifice. Ask how one today knows the right way to approach God. You might also reinforce the teaching from last week by asking what they learned about God's mercy in His dealings with Cain.
- **Introduction.** Before you even begin teaching, it would be helpful to be sure the students have before them their observation sheets for Genesis 4 and 5. They also should have lesson 26 so that they can follow and answer questions.

  You could perhaps begin this week's lesson by pretending you are a skeptic and ask the skeptic's question: 'How could the Bible be true? It says that Cain went out and found a wife. Where could he find a wife, since the Bible only tells us of Cain and Abel?' If the students don't know the answer to the question, have them go to Genesis 5:4, where it shows that Adam and Eve had other sons and daughters. In that day, there was no prohibition about marrying a close relative. Cain obviously married one of his sisters.

  Then tell them that this week we will be looking at the 'begats,' or genealogies, of big, hard-to-pronounce names. You might even ask them if they know how this can really be helpful and fun to study . . . or if they know why these genealogies are important. This lesson is supposed to tell them.
- **Class work.** Instruct the students to take out their observation sheet for Genesis 4 as well as the chart titled 'Cain and his descendants' found on page 156 of their lesson. Ask them first to follow Genesis 4:17–22 and fill in the names given in Cain's line. Then, after they complete the names, go back and read the passage again, and this time add anything they learn about each person. (While they are working, you can distribute the names of descendants you prepared. You can distribute the pictures that illustrate the descriptions of the people: city, livestock, tents, lyre, metallurgy and violence. Each student should have at least one slip of paper, if possible. Tell them they will be asked later to fasten the paper to the appropriate place on the poster board line you have placed on the wall.)

- **Discussion.** Go through the chart on Cain's line. The questions given on the second page of today's student lesson will cover what they should have learned. Use this opportunity to compare the difference in worldview concerning early man and early civilization. Ask your students what they have seen in museums and how that differs from the more advanced civilization they see in Scripture. (The seeming conflict can be settled when they understand that all archaeology and anthropology is based on post–Flood civilizations. There are no remains of pre–Flood people. There are obvious reasons why man, after coming off the Ark, would begin in a cave-dwelling, hunting-and-gathering mode. It is important for them to see that Adam, who was the first man created by God and was once free from the effects of sin, must have been an incredibly intelligent human being.)
- **Activity.** Allow students to come forward and attach their names and pictures on the poster board line you prepared for Cain (names printed in blue). As you look at the finished result, reiterate that this was the line of Cain, who went out from the presence of the Lord. His family focused on technology, on the 'good life.' But they were lost.
- **Class work.** Now direct them to their observation worksheets for chapter 5 and to the chart called 'Descendants of Adam' on the last page of their lesson. Instruct them to make another family tree, this time of the line through Seth.

  Before they begin the genealogy, direct them to Genesis 4:25–26 and the birth of Seth, with the statement that 'then men began to call upon the name of the Lord.' Help them to see that this genealogy consists of a line that began to call on the name of the LORD.

  Have them go through Genesis 5 and write the name of each descendant and the age at which each man died. (While they are working, you can distribute the slips of paper with the names of Seth's descendants {in red} as well as the slips of paper that say 'and he died at … '. They will attach them to Seth's line on the poster board after the discussion is completed.)
- **Discussion.** Go through Seth's chart with students to be sure that they have the correct answers. You might ask what differences they can see in the two family trees. (Seth's is more detailed—it mentions how long each person lived and it mentions men 'calling upon the name of the LORD,' but it doesn't say anything about technology.)

  Ask if they can guess why this genealogy is more complete than Cain's. *(because this is the line that will eventually lead to the Christ)*

  Be sure they note the repeated phrase 'and he died.' See if they can tell you the significance of that repeated word.

  Also draw the students' attention to what they learned about Enoch and the first mention of Noah.

  See if anyone can explain the apparent connection between these two lines, which go their separate ways, and the seed of the serpent and the seed of the woman talked about in Genesis 3.

If you have additional time . . .
Suggestions for augmenting lessons (home school, day school)

One extra session would enable the students to have more time to construct the genealogies of Genesis 5 as well as discuss the worldview aspects of this lesson.

Answers in Genesis has several helpful resources, including *The New Answers Book 1* (chapter 6) (available from www.AnswersInGenesis.org).

It All Begins With Genesis

LESSON 27

Events that led to God's judgment

Scripture: Genesis 6; Hebrews 11:7; 2 Peter 2:4–5

Suggested memory verse:

Genesis 6:8–9

What this lesson is about:

This lesson introduces Genesis 6. It provides further practice in the inductive study skill of 'chapter observation.' The content relates to the conditions that precipitated God's judgment by the Flood.

7 C's Connection: Corruption, Catastrophe

Goals for the lesson: The student should

- have a general understanding of the content of Genesis 6—see the progression of sin and the conditions which brought about God's judgment.
- become acquainted with Noah.
- grow in understanding inductive study skills: how to make lists from key words marked.

Preparation for lesson:

- Work through the student's lesson 27.
- Prepare Zonk game or other means for reviewing Genesis 1–5. (Some suggested questions are included at end of this lesson.)

Plan for lesson:

- **Review** last week's teaching about the two lines of humanity diverging from Adam. If you have posted the two lines as a visual, you can review by asking questions about the visual.

  You want students to understand these facts about Cain's line. They had been sent from the presence of the Lord. They became involved in material things: building cities, livestock, metallurgy, musical instruments. They became violent (Lamech). Sin was increasing.

  You want them to understand about Seth's line. It began with Seth (who was given by God to replace Abel). At this time men 'began to call upon the Lord.' They lived a long time (average 900 years) but 'they died'—the Curse was in effect. The line would continue through Noah. More detail was given about this line because it would ultimately lead to Jesus.

- **Introduction and teaching about 'sons of God.'** Instruct students to have their observation sheets for Genesis 6 and their colored pens or pencils in front of them. Tell them that the first four verses are hard to understand and disputed by biblical scholars, so you will go over the passage with them. Read together the first four verses. Then you might explain it something like this:

  Designate a group of boys in the class and tell them, 'Let's pretend you are the "sons of God." ' Identify a group of girls in the class and tell them, 'You are the "daughters of men" and you are very beautiful.' Identify another group of boys and tell them, 'You are the Nephilim. You are the "mighty men of old, men of renown." '

  The question we have to decide is 'Who are the sons of God, anyway? Who were the daughters of men? Who were the Nephilim? And why did God get so upset that He decided "enough" and sent the Flood?'

  Tell students, 'There are three different ways that biblical scholars interpret this passage. I'm going to tell you all three and then we'll see what you think is the best interpretation.' (Point to each designated group as you talk.)

  1. Since 'sons of God' is often used in the OT to mean 'angels,' it is thought that fallen angels are being described here. These bad angels left their designated place and came down to marry the human women. (Some say they came and possessed men who married the women.) The women gave birth to a kind of mongrel person who became known as Nephilim. This disobedience would have corrupted the line to Christ.

  2. Since the Bible was earlier talking about the godly line of Seth and the ungodly line of Abel, and since believers are referred to in the NT as 'sons of God,' it is possible the 'sons of God' were men from the line of Seth who married into the unbelieving line of Cain, resulting in a turning away. In this interpretation, the Nephilim might be the product of these marriages, or they might simply be another group of people, not related to the marriages.

  3. Since 'sons of God' in Scripture also refers to kings or judges, it is possible the ones who married the beautiful women were evil kings or leaders of groups outside of the line of Seth.

  After you ask for a show of hands as to the interpretation they prefer, you can add that the Bible scholars are just as divided in their ideas as they are. Then you can point out that there is an important 'bottom line' in this, and it is the same no matter what the interpretation of 'sons of God.' See if they can tell you that humans had become so terrible that God brought the Flood.

- **Class work.** Write the four key words from Genesis 6 on the board and instruct students to mark them for the whole chapter. It is usually helpful to write the symbol or color you would suggest for marking each word because it saves time waiting for them to decide how to mark it. The words are 'God,' 'Noah,' 'earth' and 'Ark.' Approximately 10 minutes are required to complete the assignment. (If you have more time than the average Sunday school, instruct them to answer all the questions in the margin of their observation sheet, and also find the theme of the chapter and draw a picture representing that theme. In most situations you will have to limit the number of observations you can make at this time.)

- **Discussion.** See if they remember why they mark key words. (Key words are repeated words in a passage. God repeats because it is important. Each key word becomes the basis for a list of what you learn from the word. You will learn something that answers a 'who, what, where, when, why or how' kind of question.)
- **Class work.** Refer students to their chart on 'key words' found in the lesson. Three words (God, Noah, earth) will be discussed today and the fourth (Ark) next week. If you have a lot of time and you think your students have already learned how to make a list, you can assign this as class work. Usually it is better to do this work together, and you write it on the board as they write it on their chart. Then when you finish, you can summarize it together. (See sample 'key words' chart at end of this lesson.)

  Name each verse (beginning with verse 3) and ask what they learned about God's thoughts and actions, about the condition of man on the earth, or about Noah.
- **Summary discussion.** As you go through all you learned about the condition of the world at Noah's time—about God's response and about His grace to Noah, you could expand on any of those themes, depending on the time you have.
- **Class work** (if time allows). If you have time, the lesson also includes two cross-references from the New Testament that give additional information about Noah. You could assign this or discuss it with the class, and add these facts about Noah to the chart on key words in the lesson.

If you have additional time . . .
Suggestions for augmenting lessons (home school, day school)

One extra session would allow more thorough observation of chapter 6 and more thorough discussion of the cross-references.

Activity. If you can save 15–20 minutes, this is a good time to review the material you have covered from the first six chapters of Genesis by playing a Zonk game. The instructions are in lesson 7, and some suggested questions are included on the following pages.

What we learn from key words in Genesis 6

God *(what He thought and did)*	3. He said His Spirit shall not strive with man forever and his days will be 120 years. (Mention that this can either mean 120 years before the Flood would come, or God was going to shorten the life spans.) 5. He saw the wickedness of men. 6. He was sorry He had made man; grieved in His heart (anthropomorphism). 7. He said He would blot out man and animals; sorry He made them. 17. He said He would send a Flood to destroy all flesh; everything on earth would perish. 18. He said He would establish His covenant with Noah.
Earth *(condition of man on the earth)*	5. The wickedness of man was great on the earth. Every intent of the thoughts of his heart was only evil continually. 11. The earth was corrupt in the sight of God; the earth was filled with violence. 12. The earth was corrupt—all flesh had corrupted their way upon earth. 13. The earth was filled with violence. 17. Everything on earth would perish.
Noah	8. Noah found favor in eyes of the Lord. 9. Noah was righteous man, blameless in His time. Noah walked with God. 10. Noah became father of three sons: Shem, Ham, Japheth 13. God told Noah He was going to destroy the earth. God told Noah to build an Ark and how to build it. 18. God told Noah that He would establish His covenant with him. 22. Noah did all that God commanded.

Zonk: Sample questions for review of Genesis 1–6

100-point questions	**What is the main event of Genesis 1?** **What is the main event of Genesis 6?** **Why did Cain kill Abel?** **What was Abel's offering? What was Cain's offering?** **What did you learn about early civilization in Genesis 4?** *(100 points for each of following: Cain built a city, dwellers in tents and livestock, metallurgy, musical instruments, violence increasing)* **Which worldview does this statement reflect, naturalistic or biblical? 'The more we study about life, the more we can see that the earth has been carefully planned for man.'** *(B)* **Naturalistic or biblical? 'Everything just exploded with a "big bang" about 15 billion years ago.'** *(N)* **Naturalistic or biblical? 'When someone is healed of cancer, it simply shows that modern medicine is making great advances.'** *(N)* **Naturalistic or biblical? 'When we look at animals, we know that there can be many kinds of dogs. But a dog could never change into a cat, or a reptile into a bird.'** *(B)* **Naturalistic or biblical? 'When we look at the layers of rocks in Grand Canyon, we can see the effects of a global Flood.'** *(B)* **Naturalistic or biblical? 'Jesus did not rise from the dead; he just swooned and later revived in the cool tomb.'** *(N)* **Naturalistic or biblical? 'When we look at the layers of rocks in Grand Canyon, we can see that it must have taken millions and millions of years for the Colorado River to form Grand Canyon.'** *(N)* **Naturalistic or biblical? 'We see evidence of intelligent design everywhere we look in nature.'** *(B)*
200-point questions	**What is the 'protoevangelium'?** *(100 points to define the meaning of the word; another 100 if they can tell where it is located in the Bible)* **How do we know God's way to do things (as opposed to *our* way)?** **What does the Bible tell us about Enoch?** *(two things: he walked with God; he was not, because God took him)* **Who was the oldest man in the world?** *(Methusaleh)* **Why do you think the genealogy of Seth's line from Adam is more detailed than Cain's line?** **What are we told about how God felt when he saw what was going on in Genesis 6?** *(grieved, sorry He made man)* **How old was Adam when he died (within 20 years)?** *(930)* **Why was Cain's offering not received by the Lord? What was wrong with it? Name at least two things.** *(his heart attitude; it was not a blood sacrifice as God had told him; it was not the 'first fruits.')*

Events that led to God's judgment

300-point questions	**What is the main event of Genesis 2?** **What is the main event of Genesis 3?** **What is the main event of Genesis 4?** **What is Genesis 5 all about?** **When was the first blood sacrifice?** **What is the difference between how someone with a naturalistic worldview and one with a biblical worldview describes early man and his civilization.** **In Genesis 4 and 5 we learn about two separate lines of civilization developing. What were they?** *(line of Cain and line of Seth)* **And how were they different?** *(line of Seth called upon the name of the Lord—led to Christ)* **What is the worst punishment anyone can receive?** *(separation from God)* **What are at least three good things we learn about Noah from Genesis 6?** **Why did God send the Flood to destroy man (give two reasons)?** *(violence, thoughts of heart evil continually, corruption)* **What is the most repeated phrase in Genesis 5?** *('and he died')*
400-point questions	**How would someone with a biblical worldview explain the presence of pain, suffering and catastrophe in the world today?** **Name two ways God showed mercy to Cain.** *(warned him, sought him out and gave time to repent, gave him a mark that kept him from being killed by others)* **There are two men named Lamech in Scripture. One was found in the line of Cain, and he was known for his vengeance and violence. The other was found in the line of Seth, and he was known because of what?** *(Noah's father)*
500-point questions	**Name three ways God showed His mercy to Adam and Eve in Genesis 3 after their sin.** **There were two men named Enoch in Genesis 4–5. One was the son of Cain, and Cain built a city for him. The other was in the line of Adam, and he was known for what?** *(walking with God, being taken by God)* **How would you explain cavemen and those who used stone tools, in the light of the Bible's teaching about early man?**

The Flood

Scripture: Genesis 6–7

Suggested memory verse:

Genesis 7:5

What this lesson is about:

This lesson is the first of three lessons on the Genesis Flood. The focus this first week will be on observing the events of chapter 7, looking particularly at the construction of the Ark and the key facts about the Flood.

7 C's Connection: Catastrophe

Goals for the lesson: The student should

- have a general understanding of the content of Genesis 6–7.
- visualize the size and construction of the Ark.

Preparation for lesson:

- Work through the student's lesson 28.
- Prepare transparencies for Genesis 7.
- Stakes (such as for tomato plants) to mark out boundaries of Noah's Ark. (Optional: A large helium balloon and string to demonstrate the height of the Ark.)
- 'Noah paraphernalia,' pictures, pins, shirts, etc.
- Read article 'Was There Really a Noah's Ark and Flood?' found at www.answersingenesis.org/go/ark-flood. A summary is found at the end of this lesson.

Plan for lesson:

- **Introduction.** You could begin by holding up some 'Noah paraphernalia' so prevalent in our culture today. There are Noah's Ark pins, mugs, lamps, shirts, towels, etc. Bring their attention to how the Flood is portrayed in our society as a boatful of cute little animals out for a sail. The effect of this propaganda is to communicate the idea that the Scriptures are fairy tales, not worthy of serious consideration. Ask the students to picture in their minds what it would really be like to have a catastrophe so serious that it blotted out all air-breathing life on earth other than that contained on the Ark.

- **Class work and discussion.** Ask the students to take out their observation sheets for Genesis 6. You might review the key words from the chapter that they marked last week. Draw their attention particularly to the word 'Ark.' Assign the questions Noah needed to know about the Ark from the first and second pages of their lesson. Discuss their answers.
- **Activity.** If time permits, a good activity would be to go outside and walk off the measurements of the Ark in the parking lot or a field outside your building. Most people are not aware that the Ark was as big as it was. Bring some stakes and stake off the four corners of the Ark. (A large helium balloon attached to a string could be used to demonstrate the height of the Ark.)
- **Class work.** Draw pictures (in the space at the top of the third page of today's student lesson). Ask for their answers to such questions as 'How could all the animals fit on the Ark?' 'How could Noah go out and find all those animals all over the world?' 'How could Noah do all that work in caring for so many animals?' You may wish to share some of this information from the article on the Ark with your students.
- **Discussion.** Ask the class if they are aware that many of the events of the Old Testament point to Jesus Christ. There are some aspects of the Flood story that foreshadow our salvation in Christ. Give them an opportunity to point out what they see, and make a list together on the board.

  Noah was saved from the judgment because he was righteous (he believed and obeyed God). We are saved because we believe in the righteousness of Christ and God's promises to us.

  The Ark was Noah's salvation from the waters of judgment. Christ is our 'Ark' of salvation from judgment.

  The Ark had only one door. Jesus is the 'Door' for our salvation.

  After the Flood, everything was 'new.' After our salvation, we are new creatures in Christ.

  God will judge sin. He did so with the Flood, and He does so now.

  God is merciful and takes care of His own.
- **Class work.** Have students begin observations of Genesis 7. If time permits, have them answer the questions from the margin of the worksheet. If time is limited, direct them to the two questions about chapter 7 given on the last page of their lesson.

Additional illustrations and activities:

- Make a bulletin board or poster that includes common questions about the Ark and their answers. You could build on this over the next three weeks.
- It would be fun to make a collection of Noah's Ark paraphernalia, borrowing samples that the children have at home, or cutting pictures from catalogs.

- A good contrast poster could be made comparing the real Ark and Flood with the mythical one of popular culture.

If you have additional time . . .
Suggestions for augmenting lessons (home school, day school)

One extra session would allow more thorough application questions related to the Ark and Jesus and would allow beginning observations of chapter 7.

Answers in Genesis has many resources available, including *The New Answers Book* (chapters 10 and 11), the videos 'Fossils and the Flood: What's the Connection?' (a 30-minute video in the series *Answers ... with Ken Ham*), *Noah's Ark: Thinking outside the Box*, and *A Jurassic Ark Mystery* (all available from www.AnswersInGenesis.org).

Was There Really a Noah's Ark and Flood? from *The New Answers Book 1* chapter 10 (www.answersingenesis.org/go/ark-flood)

> **'God Remembered Noah, and all the beasts, and all the cattle that were with him in the ark' (NAS, Genesis 8:1).**

The Ark is described as 300 cubits long, 50 cubits wide, and 30 cubits high. These dimensions are ideal according to modern studies of ship stability.

> The exact size of the cubit is unclear, being the distance from the elbow to the fingertips, but the Ark was at least 450 feet long, 75 feet wide, and 45 feet high (using a short cubit of 18 inches). It could have been as large as 510 feet by 85 feet by 51 feet (using the long cubit 0f 20.4 inches).

Ancient civilizations built boats of similar size. The exact shape of the Ark is not given in Scripture. It is possible that the traditional box shape is incorrect and that the Ark had features seen in ancient ships. The comic depections of an Ark with animals sticking out of the roof make a mockery of the true account of Scripture.

God brought the animals to Noah, he didn't have to round them up. There was plenty of room inside the Ark to accommodate all of the different kinds of animals. Only land-dwelling, air-breathing creatures were on board.

The Flood was global, covering the entire earth, with water coming from underground sources. This water receded into the ocean basins at the end of the Flood. The Flood destroyed all land-dwelling life, along with all of mankind, that was not aboard the Ark.

The voyage of the Ark

Scripture: Genesis 7–8

Suggested memory verse:

Genesis 7:11

What this lesson is about:

This lesson chronicles the events of the Flood year. It also considers whether the Flood was universal or local.

7 C's Connection: Catastrophe

Goals for the lesson: The student should

- be able to better understand the events of the Flood year, viewing them from the perspective of Captain Noah. We want the events to become real in the students' eyes.
- see from Scripture the universality of the Flood.

Preparation for lesson:

- Work through the student's lesson 29.
- Make a large wall calendar for a year plus one month. You can use old calendars and attach them to poster board. It is suggested that you begin with February and end with February the following year. You will also need a marker for noting the dates of the Flood year.

Plan for lesson:

- **Review** the key facts about the Ark and Noah that you discussed in the previous two lessons. While you are waiting for the students to arrive, you may wish to give out some paper and ask for depictions of the Ark. (You can then put them on your Genesis bulletin board under the Flood.)
- **Teaching and discussion.** Because of time constraints, it would be advisable to complete this assignment as a group, rather than individually. Ask students to take out their observation sheets for chapters 7–8, as well as their student lesson's 'Voyage of Noah's Ark log.' They will also be using colored pens or pencils.

  Ask a teacher assistant to help by being ready to mark the pertinent dates and comments on the wall calendar as the discussion proceeds. If you don't have a helper, you can do this yourself.

  Display the observation sheet for chapter 7 (on the curriculum CD). Tell the students you are most interested in the time statements in these chapters, and that you will be marking them (with a little colored clock) whenever you see something that tells you about time. Then begin reading chapter 7 together, stopping when you want to note something in particular. Break the discussion down into the various time segments, and have the students draw lines across the observation sheet to indicate the different segments. After you discuss the text with them, help them to fill in their ship's log that they have in their lesson. Tell them you want them to be imagining at each step of the way what it would have been like.

The following chart should help you lead this discussion (italics show what is already written in the student outline).

The voyage of Noah's Ark

Scripture	Date	What happened
Genesis 7:1–9 Instruct students to draw a line after verse 9. Read 1–9, marking verses 4 and 6 with time clocks. Note Noah's obedience in verse 5.	February 10—write this date on the calendar: 'Noah and family enter Ark. God shuts door.' *Noah was 600 years old. Waited on the Ark for 7 days.* You might ask if they remember how old Noah was when he had his children (500)—so how old (approximately) would Shem, Ham and Japheth be at this time?	*God told us to enter the Ark with all the animals. We obeyed and waited 7 days.* *God closed the door.* (How would you feel if you were on that Ark waiting for something to happen? Possible log: 'Scary people jeering outside—felt kind of silly.')

Scripture	Date	What happened
Genesis 7:10–8:3 Instruct students to draw a line after 8:3. This section tells you about the Flood itself. Read together, marking the time indicators on the observation sheet. Since verses 10–12 are so important, have students put a big box around that section. Tell them we'll come back to that in two weeks.	February 17—write on the calendar: 'Flood begins.' March 28—end of 40 days and nights period. *In the 600th year of Noah's life, in the second month, on the 17th day of the month*	*All fountains of the great deep burst open …* Floodgates of sky opened: rained 40 days and nights. Water increased and Ark lifted up. Water prevailed and increased greatly. All high mountains everywhere under the heavens covered. All flesh on dry land perished. Water prevailed 150 days. God remembered Noah and sent wind, and the water subsided and receded steadily. (Discuss what it would have been like during that time. Possible log: 'People screaming to be let into the Ark. Incessant rain 40 days.' Boredom? Fear?)
Genesis 8:4–5a Draw a line after verse 5a. Read the verse and mark time indicators.	*7th month, 17th day of the month* July 17—write on calendar: 'Ark rests on mountains of Ararat.'	Ark rested on the mountains of Ararat. Water decreased steadily. (What would it have been like? 'Yes! This is the first time in over 5 months that we haven't been floating!')
Genesis 8:5b Draw a line after verse 8:5. Read verse and mark time indicators.	*10th month, 1st day of the month* October 1—write on calendar: 'Tops of mountains become visible.'	Mountains became visible. (What would it have been like? 'Three more months of sitting there waiting for water to go down. It was *exciting* when we finally saw the tops of the mountains!')

The voyage of the Ark

Scripture	Date	What happened
Genesis 8:6–9 Draw a line after verse 8:9. Read verses and mark time indicators.	*40 days later* November 10—write on the calendar: 'Send out raven and dove. Dove returns.'	Noah opened the window of the Ark and sent out a raven that did not return. Then he sent out a dove, which returned. (This means the raven could feast on dead carcasses, but the dove needed vegetation and couldn't find it. So the ground was still covered with water.)
Genesis 8:10–11 Draw a line after 8:11. Mark time indicators.	*7 days later* November 17—write on the calendar: 'Dove sent out, returns with olive leaf.'	Sent out dove again. Came back with an olive leaf. ('Olive trees are growing again—cool! But perhaps the dove didn't have enough vegetation to support life or perhaps there still was no dry place to land.')
Genesis 8:12 Draw a line after 8:12. Mark time indicator.	*7 days later* November 24—mark on the calendar: 'Dove sent out—does not return.'	Sent out dove again. This time she did not come back. ('Yes! So now when can we get off this thing? We have to wait on the Lord.')
Genesis 8:13 Draw a line after 8:13. Mark time indicator.	*In the 601st year, in the first month, on the first day of the month* January 1—mark on the calendar: 'Removed covering of Ark; ground dried up.'	Water dried up from earth. Noah removed the covering of the Ark and looked, and the surface of the ground was dried up. ('And still we wait till the Lord says it is time to get off.')
Genesis 8:14–22 Draw a line at verse 22 (end of chapter).	*In the second month, on the 27th day* February 27—mark on calendar: 'God tells Noah to leave Ark.'	God tells Noah to leave Ark. Noah builds altar and sacrifices/worships. God says He'll never again curse the ground as He has done; rainbow is a sign. ('We have been on the Ark more than a year—now we begin a new, scary life. But God is with us. What are some of the challenges we will face?')

- **Class work and discussion.** Ask the class, 'Did the Flood cover the entire earth, or was it a local event?' Tell them that many people question the universality of the Flood. So our job today is to look more closely at Scripture and see what it says. Assign Genesis 7:19–24 and have them circle in red the universal language ('all' and 'every'). Go over their assignment and ask them what they learned.
- **Discuss** the universality of the Flood issue. There is an article included at the end of this lesson guide that gives you more information to discuss with your students.

If you have additional time . . .
Suggestions for augmenting lessons (home school, day school)

One extra session would be helpful.

You could allow more individual work in completing the diary of Noah, and the extra time would allow more discussion of the issue of a worldwide vs local Flood.

The extent of the Flood: Does Scripture teach a global Deluge?

Importance of the issue

Henry Morris clearly states in *The Genesis Record* (p. 198) the importance of the issue to the Christian church:

'The question of the nature and historicity of the Noahic Deluge is of immense importance to biblical Christianity. The fact of the Flood is a pivotal issue in the entire conflict between Christianity and anti-Christianity. If the principle of innate evolutionary development can fully explain the universe and all its inhabitants, as its proponents claim, then there is no need to postulate a Creator. The chief evidence for evolution is the geological record of the supposed billions of years of earth history, documented by the fossils entombed in the sedimentary rocks of the earth's crust; and there is no room in this framework of interpretation for a world-destroying Flood. Thus, if the latter has actually occurred, the assumptions of uniformity and evolution as guiding principles in interpreting earth history are thereby proved completely deceptive and false.

'In our modern age of scientific skepticism, the enormity of this great event of the past has been all but forgotten. Its testimony of the awfulness of sin and the reality of divine retribution is so disturbingly unwelcome that men have tried for ages somehow to explain it away and forget it.'

Scriptural evidence for a global Deluge

If Scripture indeed teaches that the Flood was a worldwide cataclysm, then it follows that this fact should be foundational to all our interpretations of the world around us. The following are cited as biblical evidence for a worldwide Flood:

1. **The biblical explanation of the initiation of the Flood.** In Genesis 7:11 we read, 'All the fountains of the great deep burst open and the floodgates of the sky were opened.' It seems obvious that, whatever the exact mechanism was for the initiation of the Flood, it involved great sea-floor disturbances that could not conceivably have resulted in a mere local catastrophe.
2. **The depth of the Flood.** In Genesis 7:19 we read, 'The water prevailed more and more upon the earth so that all the high mountains everywhere under the heavens were covered.' The use of the double superlative and the description that all mountains everywhere under the heavens can only be understood in the universal sense.
3. **The duration of the Flood.** The Flood covered all the mountains in 6 weeks and continued to cover all the high mountains for an additional 16 weeks. 150 days after the onset, the waters started to subside, and the Ark was grounded on the mountain. Ten weeks after being grounded on the mountain, nothing could be seen except other mountain peaks. Another 21 weeks was required before Noah could disembark, still in the mountains of Ararat. How a Flood of such depth and duration could have covered only a limited portion of the earth's surface has never been satisfactorily explained.

4. **The need for an Ark.** There would have been no need for an Ark at all if the Flood was local. The whole procedure of constructing such a vessel, involving over 100 years of work (Genesis 6:3) to escape a local flood is absurd. God could have merely warned Noah of the coming destruction in plenty of time for him to move to an area that would not have been affected by the Flood. The animals could have migrated out of the danger zone also, rather than enduring a year in a barge.

5. **The total destruction of a widely distributed human race.** It has been generally accepted throughout history by conservative Christian scholars that the Flood must have destroyed the entire human race because the purpose of the Flood was to wipe out a sinful and degenerate humanity, and repeatedly statements are made in Scripture that Noah and his family were the only ones who escaped. Many who assert the above contend that the Flood was local in a geographical sense, but that mankind was not distributed widely at this time.

However, there are many indications that the human race was widely distributed by this time. The remarkable longevity of the antediluvians imply a rapid increase of population during the minimum of 1,656 years that elapsed between Adam and the Flood. The prevalence of strife and violence suggests wide distribution of peoples ('The earth was filled with violence,' Genesis 6:11).

6. **Use of Hebrew word '*mabbul*' and Greek word '*kataklusmos*' for the Flood.** These words are used solely in connection with the Noahic Flood. The ordinary Hebrew or Greek words for a local flood are not used here at all.

7. **The covenant of the rainbow.** (Genesis 8:21; 9:11, 15) God promised never to send such a Flood again. This promise has been broken repeatedly if only a local flood occurred.

8. **Testimony of the Apostle Peter in 2 Peter 3:3–7.** Peter spoke of a day when men would no longer think seriously of Christ's Second Coming as a cataclysmic, universal intervention by God into the course of world affairs. The reason for this would be a blind adherence to the doctrine of total uniformitarianism, a doctrine that maintains that natural laws and processes have never yet been interrupted so as to bring about a total destruction of human civilization through the direct intervention of God. Peter pointed to two events in the past: the Creation of the world and the Flood. Peter was clearly speaking of the destruction of the earth in the universal sense and in cosmic terms.

9. **The use of universal terms.** Expressions involving universality occur more than 30 times in Genesis 6–9. It is true that terms like 'all' and 'every' need not be understood in the strictly universal sense. The only possible way to determine the sense in which universal terms are to be understood is to examine the immediate and general context in which they are used. Genesis 1–11 deals with universal origins: Creation, sin, redemption, judgment, nations. When the context limits the meaning of universal terms, they must not be understood in the absolutely universal sense. When the context does not limit the meaning, they almost certainly are to be understood in the absolute sense.

10. **The Lord Jesus Christ accepted the historicity and universality of the Flood.** See Matthew 24:37–39; Luke 17:26, 27. He made it the climactic sign and type of the coming worldwide judgment when He returns.

For further information (available from www.AnswersInGenesis.org)

J. Whitcomb, *The World that Perished*, Baker Book House, Grand Rapids, Michigan, 1973.

H. Morris, *The Genesis Record*, Baker Book House, Grand Rapids, Michigan, 1976.

It All Begins With Genesis

LESSON 30

Dinosaurs and the Flood

Scripture: Job 40:15–24; 41:1–34; Genesis 1, 6 and 7 (assorted verses)

Suggested memory verse:

Job 40:15a

What this lesson is about:

This lesson looks at the popular question of dinosaurs and how they fit into biblical history. In our culture, dinosaurs are often used to teach evolutionary theory. This lesson seeks to give children a biblical worldview concerning the fascinating subject of dinosaurs.

7 C's Connection: Creation, Corruption, Catastrophe

Goals for the lesson: The student should

- see how dinosaurs fit into the biblical account of Creation and the Flood.
- note the appearance of great dinosaur-like beasts in Scripture.
- be able to give biblical and reasonable answers to frequently asked dinosaur questions.
- be able to differentiate between the biblical and naturalistic view of dinosaurs.

Preparation for lesson:

- Work through the student's lesson 30.
- This lesson is shorter than some lessons. You might want to use this opportunity to add a short game of Zonk in order to review the past lessons. There are some dinosaur videos you could also use to augment the lesson. *Dinosaurs and the Bible* and *The Riddle of the Dinosaurs* are videos available from Answers in Genesis. Dr. Kurt Wise also has a very good segment on dinosaurs (15 minutes) in his Precept upon Precept *Genesis Part 2* lectures. It is lesson 8 on "The Flood, the Ark, the Dinosaurs."
- You may wish to bring to the class some Bibles in different English versions in order to point out their marginal notes for Job 40 and 41. Illustrations 30-1–5 (on the curriculum CD) show a humorous depiction of the cedar tree tail on various animals.
- There are some helpful books available, written from a biblical perspective. They include *Dinosaurs by Design* by Duane Gish, *The Great Dinosaur Mystery and the Bible* by Paul Taylor, and *Dinosaurs for Kids* by Ken Ham (all available from www.Answers-InGenesis.org). You could also pick up some dinosaur books from the library that are

written from a naturalistic worldview, and begin the class with an excerpt from one of those books.

- You can use your worldview eyeglasses.

Plan for lesson:

- **Introduction.** Hold up a colorful dinosaur book (written from an evolutionary perspective) and read a passage from the book that teaches evolution. Or you could play a section from a video on dinosaurs that presents an evolutionary view (such as *Jurassic Park* or *Land Before Time*). Ask the students if they have ever wondered how a Christian should understand dinosaurs. You might ask them for questions they have, and then write them on the board for discussion later as they are covered during the lesson.

- **Class work.** Direct students to the first question: Are dinosaurs found in the Bible? Be sure to teach about the recent origin of the word 'dinosaur.' Then write *behemoth* on the board. Assign the Job 40 passage in their workbooks and ask them to highlight what they read about behemoth. Before the assignment, be sure they understand something of the context of Job—that the book was written in the early centuries following the Flood.

- **Discussion.** As you discuss their observations of Job 40, you could distribute several different modern translations of the Bible, and ask a student to read the marginal note for Job 40:15. This is a good opportunity to point out that even good biblical scholars can adopt naturalistic views of the world.

  *I*llustrations 30-1 through 30–5 depict what a 'tail like a cedar' looks like if placed on an elephant or a hippopotamus or a dinosaur. You may wish to point out that the 'cedar' referred to in the passage is not the scrawny cedar most of us have seen, but rather huge trees like the cedars of Lebanon, used to build the temple.

- **Class work and discussion.** Now write *leviathan* on the board. Assign Psalm 104:26 and Job 41. Discuss what students observed about leviathan.

- **Class work and discussion.** Finally, write *tannin* on the board and direct students to the verses given. It would probably be good to do this section together. *Tannin* is interesting because it is included often in Scripture and is translated with many different English meanings. In the three examples given, it is translated 'sea monster' and 'serpent.' In the King James Version it is usually translated 'dragon.' Again, this illustrates the naturalistic presuppositions even among Bible translators.

- **Class work and discussion**. Give the class time to work through the questions on page 4: 'When did God create dinosaurs?' *(They are land animals, created on Day 6.)* 'Did dinosaurs go on the Ark?' *(Yes, all air breathing land animals went on Ark.)* What happened to the dinosaurs after the Flood? *(They died out. They primarily ate gymnosperm plants, which were not plentiful* *following the Flood. Also, they were probably hunted and exterminated by man following the Flood. Climate changes and post-Flood catastrophes also may have played a part.)* You might mention that there have been reports of dinosaur sightings in recent years, so it is possible a few still exist.

- **Discussion.** After you discuss the answers to the common dinosaur questions, bring out your different kinds of eyeglasses and make the contrast between the naturalistic and biblical view of dinosaurs.

  Naturalistic view of dinosaurs: Dinosaurs evolved from amphibians and later into birds. They became extinct 60 millions of years before man evolved. We do not know why or how they became extinct (a wide variety of theories have been proposed).

  Biblical view of dinosaurs: Dinosaurs were created on Day 6 of Creation, the same Day as man. They coexisted with man prior to the Flood, although probably not in the same area. They were created as herbivores, but after the Fall many became carnivorous. They were created according to their kind and exhibit intelligent design. Representatives were taken on the Ark along with the other land animals (probably juveniles) and they left the Ark when the other animals left. Many were destroyed in the floodwaters, and their remains are found plentifully in Flood sediments today. The surviving creatures probably had a difficult time making it after the Flood. Their favorite kind of plant was no longer plentiful. Climactic changes and other catastrophes occurred following the Flood. Furthermore, man may have hunted them for food in those early post–Flood years. They eventually became extinct. A few may still survive in remote areas today.

If you have additional time . . .
Suggestions for augmenting lessons (home school, day school)

Although the lesson can be completed in one session, adding one session would allow more depth in looking at supplementary materials and answering questions. *The New Answers Book 1* (chapter 12) provides additional information on dinosaurs as well as the video *Dinosaurs and the Bible* (both available from www.AnswersInGenesis.org). You may also wish to use Dr Wise's excellent lecture on "The Ark, the Flood and the Dinosaurs" to augment the entire series of Flood lectures. It is lecture 8 of the *Genesis Part 2* Precept course.

It All Begins With Genesis — LESSON 31

Is there evidence of a worldwide Flood?

Scripture: Genesis 7:11; Psalm 104:6–9; 2 Peter 3:3–7

Suggested memory verse (choose one):

2 Peter 3:5–6; Psalm 104:8–9

What this lesson is about:

This lesson contrasts the naturalistic and biblical worldviews concerning the rocks and fossils. It attempts to help the students see that ample evidence for a worldwide Flood surrounds us today, and it challenges students to see why our interpretation of the rock record makes a difference in our worldview.

Note: This lesson is primarily a geology lesson. Interest and ability to understand this material will differ widely. Most 6th and 7th graders have little understanding of earth science. Furthermore, many adults have never studied geology. The concepts presented in this lesson may also challenge you, the teacher.

Please feel free to greatly modify this lesson according to the students' ability and interest and your confidence in the subject.

It should be your goal to answer the three questions listed below. However, you may answer each in a simplified manner. Some portions of the lesson will be marked 'optional.'

7 C's Connection: Catastrophe

Goals for the lesson: The student should

- be able to answer three questions about the Genesis Flood:
    1. Where did the water come from?
    2. What happened during the Flood?
    3. Where did all the floodwaters go?
- be able to explain the difference between the naturalistic and biblical ways of looking at the rocks and fossils of the world.
- see something of the character of God in the midst of judgment.

Preparation for lesson:

- Work through the student's lesson 31.

- Read the article 'Catastrophic Plate Tectonics' found at the end of this lesson plan.
- Props needed:

  Something to illustrate the core, mantle and crust of the earth. (Suggested: an apple)

  (Optional) Something to represent continental and oceanic crust of the earth. (Suggested: green play dough for continental crust and thinly rolled blue play dough for oceanic crust. OR—use flat section of Styrofoam to represent continental crust and aluminum foil to represent oceanic crust.)

  Something to represent how sedimentary rock layers form. (Suggested: several different kinds of bread. OR—use different colors of rice or sand layered in a container.)
- Illustrations of fossil facts (included at the end of this lesson)
- 'Billions of dead things' song on the *Creation Songs* CD by Buddy Davis, available from Answers in Genesis (see www.AnswersInGenesis.org)
- Worldview eyeglasses: naturalistic and biblical

Plan for lesson:

- **Introduction.** Ask the students what one with a naturalistic worldview would say about a global Flood in history. *(It is myth, a children's story.)* Ask them what many Christians would say about the worldwide Flood in the time of Noah. *(It was only a local Flood.)* Tell them that today you want to help give them some evidence that indeed a worldwide Flood is a historical reality and help them to answer the skeptics' challenges to this point of view.
- **Teaching and class work.** *Question 1. Where did all the water come from?* Point the students to Genesis 7:11, the most descriptive verse of what happened during the Flood, and have them fill in the blanks. Then discuss the meaning of 'fountains of the great deep' (the Flood probably originated in the bottom of the ocean) and floodgates of the sky.

  Pose the dilemma given on the second page of today's student lesson. (If all the water were wrung out of all the clouds, the sea level would only be raised about ½ inch.) So, since the water couldn't have come from the clouds only, where could it come from? Ask them to come up with an idea and write it in the blank given. (They will probably suggest that either the land sunk down or the ocean rose in order to allow the oceans to cover the land.)

  Teaching: the internal structure of the earth. Direct the class to the drawing on the second page of their lesson. It would be helpful if you cut a real apple in half to point out the crust, mantle and core of the earth. Then, using your knife, cut the skin of the apple into 'plates' to give a simple explanation of plate tectonics. (Note: The back of this lesson discusses a catastrophic plate tectonics model for the Flood. It has far more detail than you could hope to discuss in class, but it might help you to understand the concepts better.)

Teaching: the plates of the earth. (**Optional Material**. Read through this section, but feel free to omit if sufficient interest, time and understanding are not present. Instead, substitute a simple discussion of how the plates of the earth have been moving slowing during the present time, but possibly moved very quickly at the time of the Flood. The huge amount of water that covered the continents during the Flood was probably produced not only by massive global rain but also by ocean floor disturbances that caused the ocean waters to cover the continents. There are also many resources available on the Answers in Genesis website.)

Point to the map with the plates, shown on the third page of today's lesson. Tell students that there are two kinds of plates that make up the crust: the continental and the oceanic. Use two green pieces of play dough to illustrate the continental plates. Explain that these are mostly granite and are less dense than the oceanic plates. (Explain what *density* means—these would be more like marshmallows as opposed to hard cheese.) The continental plates 'float' above the mantle because they are not as dense. Then use two pieces of blue play dough, the oceanic plates. These are made of basalt (like lava) and are denser than the continental plates. They sink down into the mantle and form the ocean basins that hold the water. (Another idea: use two flat pieces of Styrofoam for the continental plates and two sheets of aluminum foil for the oceanic plates.)

Then go through the way plates apparently relate to each other (use illustration on the third page of the student's lesson).

1. When similar plates converge (come together), they form mountains, such as the Rockies and Himalayas. (Use the two pieces of play dough to show them coming together and forming mountains.)

2. When plates diverge (pull apart), magma comes up to make new ocean floor. (Illustrate.) The Mid-Atlantic Ridge is an example.

3. When an ocean plate meets a continental plate, the ocean plate subducts (dives) under the continental plate. Lava comes up here also, and volcanoes often form. The ocean plate subducts because it is denser than the continental plate.

4. When plates move or slide laterally against each other, earthquakes result.

Ask how fast these plates are moving today (inches per year). Ask if students can visualize a time when they moved very quickly, such as meters per second. Illustrate the creationist model of 'runaway subduction,' using the clay. (The ocean crust took a dive under the continental crust, the movement becoming more and more rapid, resulting in the entire ocean crust diving down deep into the mantle. This would cause continents to bump into each other because they are less dense and would not be pulled down. It would also allow mantle to come to the surface. The hot mantle hitting the cold ocean would result in geyser-like activity and would precipitate heavy rainfall. Also, because the hot mantle is less dense than the original ocean floor, the waters of the ocean would then overflow the land.) Stress that this is one model—there are other models under consideration. But the model is reasonable and it also explains other facts, such as the cold material detected near the core of the earth, and the fact that the sediments of the ocean floor are considered to be younger, post-Flood sediments.

Class work. Ask the students to summarize the description of the tectonic Flood model in the place provided in the middle of page 179. As they give you their summary, you may wish to write it on the board for them. It should include something like:

> Rapid subduction of the ocean crust under the crust of the continents. Ocean crust was replaced with less dense, hot mantle. The result was geysers and heavy rain, and the oceans were able to cover the land.

- **Teaching and illustration.** *Question 2. What happened during the Flood?* Direct the students to the third page of their lesson and the illustration of sedimentary strata.

Give each group of six students some slices of bread, different colors and types. Tell them the bread will illustrate the sediments that were transported around by the floodwaters. Have them begin to place each layer on the green play dough (representing the continental granite basement rocks). Your narrative could go something like this:

> The Flood is beginning, and new ocean currents are transporting ocean sediments. The water is moving very fast. Many sea-bottom animals are buried, while others that are more mobile can escape. (Place one slice of bread on the play dough.)
>
> The floodwaters continue to rise and sediments come in quickly. Bottom-dwelling fish are overcome and buried as sudden influxes of sediment come in. Wow, look at all those fish getting buried! (Place a contrasting color of bread on the previous slice.)
>
> Here come more sediments from another direction. The little amphibians and reptiles just can't escape any longer. They are buried at this time of the Flood. (Add another slice.)
>
> As the Flood continues, the waters cover other life zones, and the larger dinosaurs and reptiles are buried. They can escape no longer (another slice).

Ask them if they have ever seen rocks in layers like these layers of bread.

Teaching about fossils. Obviously, included in all those sediments were the remains of billions of dead things—fossils. Some helpful facts about fossils are included at the back of this lesson. They can be used as illustrations for presentation. You also may want to play a song by Buddy Davis (recording artist with *Answers in Genesis*) called 'Billions of dead things.'

- **Teaching and illustration.** *Question 3. Where did all the floodwaters go?*

Class work. Assign Psalm 104:6–9, found on the fourth page of the student's lesson. Ask students to find the verse in the psalm that might suggest what happened to the waters that covered the continents.

Illustration. Use the bread sedimentary layers to show how metamorphic rock can modify the sedimentary rocks (step on it or twist it) and how it was twisted and tilted by forces at the close of the Flood. Many geology books have dramatic photos of twisted strata.

Ask next what happens to land that lies below a dam when that dam bursts or water overflows it. (Erosion would occur—canyon formation. This can be illustrated by using a water hose directed across a sandbox, although this would be difficult to accomplish in a church setting.) Creationists witnessed amazing canyon formation at the Mount St Helens eruption, when mudflows and other volcanic flows cut through the sediments in the area. Could similar (but greater) processes have formed Grand Canyon?

- **Summary discussion.** Ask the students if they can say what all this 'science' stuff has to teach about God. What spiritual lessons are learned by looking at the Flood? (They may see something of the character of God: His power, His work in judgment.)

  You would also want to direct them to lessons about mankind. Why do men resist the teaching of the Flood?

  Close by reading 2 Peter 3 and ask what they see about those who deny the Creation and the Flood. (They are *willfully* ignorant. They wear naturalistic eyeglasses. They don't want to recognize God's power and righteous judgment.)

Other suggested supplementary material (available from Answers in Genesis, see www.AnswersInGenesis.org)

- At present there is little supplementary material written to explain catastrophic plate tectonics at the lay level. This is a relatively new theory, and more help will be coming in the future.
- A powerful video describes the Mount Saint Helens volcanic catastrophe, effectively demonstrating how strata and canyons form quickly. It is an hour long, so an extra week would be required if you want to show it. The video is produced by the Institute for Creation Research and is called *Mount Saint Helens: Explosive Evidence for Catastrophe.*
- Another excellent video produced by the Institute for Creation Research is called *Grand Canyon: Monument to Catastrophe.*
- Answers in Genesis offers many video resources on geology including *Flood Geology* and the *Geology* series by Dr. Andrew Snelling.

If you have additional time . . .
Suggestions for augmenting lessons (home school, day school)

One or more extra sessions would be helpful. This material integrates well with earth science class and the subject of plate tectonics, as well as material on the fossil record.

Dr. Kurt Wise's lecture 9 "Physical Evidence for the Flood" found in the Precept *Genesis Part 2* course is excellent for mature students.

The other videos suggested as 'supplementary material' (previous page) are also excellent to increase understanding.

A look at a global Flood model of earth history:

CATASTROPHIC PLATE TECTONICS

by Sheila Richardson and Dr Kurt P. Wise

Biblical basis for the model

The biblical creationist builds his scientific models on the foundation of Scripture. The biblical foundation laid in Genesis 1 and 7 is the basis for the model described in this article. In the opening chapters of Genesis, we are given some truths that might lead us to the answers to two basic questions.

1. How did the ocean basins and continents form?

'Then God said "Let the waters below the heavens be gathered into one place and let the dry land appear" ' (Genesis 1:9).

On Day 3 of Creation, the ocean lows and the continent highs were formed.

2. Did a seafloor upheaval cause Noah's Flood?

'In the six hundredth year of Noah's life, in the second month, on the seventeenth day of the month, on the same day all the fountains of the great deep burst open and the floodgates of the sky were opened … . And the water prevailed more and more upon the earth so that all the high mountains everywhere under the heavens were covered' (Genesis 7:11, 19).

This passage suggests that the Flood began in the ocean, rains followed, and by the time it ended, all the high hills under the whole heaven were covered with water. It may be that the bursting action of the ocean floor began the chain of events that resulted in the global cataclysm.

What is 'plate tectonics'? Have the continents really moved apart?

Before describing the model, it would be helpful to discuss the subject of plate tectonics in general.

In 1859, a creationist named Antonio Snider proposed that all the continents were originally gathered together in one landmass and that crustal plates moved catastrophically during the Genesis Flood. However, his ideas were not considered or were readily dismissed. Darwin's *Origin of Species* had been published the same year, and the idea of uniformitarian geology (slow processes over much time), as introduced by Hutton and Lyell, had taken hold.

For many years following, most geologists strongly held that the continents were stationary. However, beginning in the second decade of this century, a change in thought began. This change was accelerated in the 1960's as a result of scientific studies involving the mapping of the seafloors, the measuring of magnetic fields and greater understanding of earthquakes through seismometers. Plate tectonics as a model of earth history was becoming accepted.

Basically, this is what the plate tectonics theory claims:

- The earth's surface crust consists of a mosaic of rigid plates, each moving with respect to its adjacent plates.
- The geologic activity that occurs along plate boundaries differs according to the way plates move in relation to each other. There are basically three types of motion involved:
    1. Two plates *move apart* from one another. (This is called a 'divergent boundary.') As they move apart, molten rock from the mantle below rises and fills the space between the plates. As the molten rock cools, it hardens onto the edges of the separating plates and creates new oceanic crust (for example, the Mid-Atlantic Ridge and East Pacific Rise).
    2. Two plates *move toward* one another. (This is called a 'convergent boundary.') If the colliding plates are both made of continental crust, the colliding edges are crumpled and uplifted, producing large linear mountain ranges (e.g. the Himalayas and the Alps). If an oceanic plate is involved, the result will be subduction of the oceanic crust (a sinking under the other plate). A deep trench forms as one of the plates is subducted under the other, and molten rock from the sinking plate rises to the surface along the far side of the trench to form a chain of volcanoes (or volcanic islands, if oceanic crust is there).
    3. Two plates are adjacent to and *slip past* one another. (This is called a 'transform fault boundary.') When two plates are grinding past each other, the plate edges usually do not slide along smoothly. Instead, they scrape together and move in sudden spurts of activity (for example, the San Andreas fault in California).

It is generally accepted that a single supercontinent broke apart, with continental pieces moving apart to their current locations. This idea is based in part on the apparent fit of the eastern bulge of South America into the southwestern concavity of Africa, the corresponding correlation of the rock strata systems, and the fold mountains found in North America and Western Europe.)

Because uniformitarian evolutionary assumptions have been the basis for twentieth-century geology, plate tectonics theory suggests plates have always moved very slowly—about two to eighteen centimeters per year. At that rate, it would require 100-million years to form an ocean basin or mountain range.

What then is 'catastrophic plate tectonics'?

It is well established now that the continents have moved in the past, but it is not clear whether measurements of slow motion observed today represent the kind of motion for all time past, or are simply minor readjustments.

Dr John Baumgardner, working at the Los Alamos National Laboratory, has demonstrated from supercomputer modeling of processes in the earth's mantle that plate tectonics/continental drift can occur catastrophically.[1] His research has provided the foundation for a catastrophic plate tectonics global Flood model for earth history that is able to explain more geological data than the conventional plate tectonics model, with its millions of years.

The pre-Flood earth

We must begin with a basic understanding of the pre-Flood earth, which we think contained a core, mantle and crust much as we have today. The *core*, the center of the earth, is very dense—probably from iron and nickel. It is the area from which we believe the magnetic field emanates. The core is divided into a solid inner core and a liquid outer core. The *mantle*, making up 70% of the volume of the earth, is made of solid silicate rocks, which amazingly have the property of behaving plastically under certain types of stress. The *crust*, the very thin outer shell, today consists of rocks of two different types—continental and oceanic. The continental crust is predominately granitic rocks, while the oceanic crust is predominantly basaltic. The continental crust is of lower density (i.e. lesser compactness), enabling it to 'float' well above the oceanic crust. Ocean water fills in the area over the lower oceanic crust, leaving the continental crust exposed above sea level. Because there was both dry land and ocean from Day 3 of the Creation Week on, it is assumed continental and oceanic crust existed in the pre-Flood world very much as they do today.

'God slammed the door of the Ark'

It is not known what initiated the Flood. Many ideas have been suggested, including asteroid or comet hits, such as we see in many popular 'doomsday' movies today. The earth may have been so prepared for the Flood that it may not have taken much to set it in motion. Perhaps it is more than coincidence that when God slammed the door of the Ark, the Flood began!

According to the tectonic model, three events happened simultaneously and rapidly at the beginning of the Flood. (Try to picture in your mind the three events happening at the same time.)

1. **The ocean crust 'takes a dive.'**

   Visualize for a moment the area where the ocean crust and the continental crust come together. Remember, the crust of the continents is lighter and 'floats' above the mantle, while the ocean crust is more dense, or compact, and sinks into the mantle. At the onset of the Flood, the ocean crust broke loose from the continental crust and began to dip into the mantle (this is called *subduction*). As oceanic crust broke loose, it dipped down along thousands of kilometers of pre-Flood continental margins. As it dove, it deformed the mantle material. The friction and deformation caused the temperature of the mantle material to increase, resulting in the material itself becoming thinner, speeding up the process. (Have you ever cooked with honey? Note how, when honey becomes warm, it becomes thinner and pours faster, but when it is cold it is very thick. The crustal material dipping into the mantle experiences the same type of phenomenon.) In catastrophic plate tectonics theory it is thought that the sinking plates sped up until they dove into the mantle at meters per second. This is called *runaway subduction.*

Next, picture what happened to the continents that were still attached to the other end of those runaway ocean plates. Those continents would be pulled across the earth's surface towards the subduction zones at meters per second. Since the continental crust is lighter, once it got to the subduction zone it would not be pulled all the way into the mantle, but the continent would have been taken on quite a ride, nevertheless! As a result of this, continents would have broken up, continents would have collided, and enormous waves, earthquakes and volcanoes would have resulted. It is believed that essentially *all* pre-Flood ocean floor was subducted into the mantle during the course of the Flood. (All current ocean crust and sediments seem to date from Flood or post-Flood times.)

2. **The entire mantle and core of the earth experiences motion and change.**

   As the oceanic crust dipped into the mantle, other processes were set in motion. Mantle material pushed out of the way by subducting crust would have to go *somewhere!* Computer simulations suggest large-scale flow was induced throughout the entire mantle of the earth. (Seismic tomography studies seem to confirm that has happened during the history of the earth.) Ultimately, the entire ocean floor was pulled down toward the core/mantle boundary. Even before the crust made it to the base of the mantle, cooler mantle material moved downward and would have cooled the outer core (which is a liquid) in an uneven way. This uneven cooling would then initiate circulation patterns in the outer core.

   We know from studying magnetic fields that magnetic field lines are 'tied' to the substance they are passing through. We also know (from generators, for example) that moving magnetic field lines generate a changing electric current. And, when one has a changing electric current, a magnetic field weaker than the original field is created and it points in the opposite direction from the first magnetic field. Thus, when the cooler mantle material caused core circulation, magnetic field lines carried in that circulating material would generate a weaker magnetic field oriented in the opposite direction from the earth's main field. This reversed field is transmitted to the outside of the earth and is perceived on the surface as a *magnetic field reversal.* Field reversals, and reversals of reversals, could happen very quickly in this model. This model predicted that rapid magnetic field reversals might be found in a single layer of the 'proper' thickness of cooling lava, and *this prediction has been confirmed.*

3. **The rains come down and the waters cover the land.**

   As the pre-Flood ocean floor dipped down into the mantle, it was rapidly replaced by hot material from the mantle, and a new ocean floor was created by the spreading magma. The hot material coming from below, as it contacted the cold ocean, would have vaporized ocean water to produce a linear geyser of superheated gases along the whole length of spreading material (a geyser effect—possibly 'the fountains of the great deep'?). As it cooled, the water—both the water that vaporized from ocean water and the water that released from magma—would have fallen as an intense global rain. It is this geyser-produced rain that is believed to be primarily responsible for the rain from the 'windows of heaven,' which remained a source of water for up to 150 days of the Flood (Genesis 7:24; 8:2).

   But, how then were the high mountains all over the earth covered with water?

If water simply evaporated from the ocean and fell back in again, sea level would remain unchanged. In the catastrophic plate tectonics model, the warmer new ocean floor was less dense (less compacted) than the old ocean floor it replaced. This would serve to raise the ocean floor along the spreading centers. This produced a linear chain of mountains called the mid-ocean ridge system. The warmer and more buoyant ocean floor displaced ocean water onto the continents to produce the inundation itself.

The end of the Flood

The events of the Flood would have made substantial modification and unevenness to the thickness of the pre-Flood continental crust. Sediments were redistributed, and new molten material was added. Large-scale adjustments would follow: enormous earthquake activity, mountain formation and extensive volcanism. (Tens of thousands of volcanoes have been found on the Pacific seafloor.)

When virtually all the pre-Flood oceanic floor had been replaced with new, less-dense, less-subductable rock, rapid plate motion ceased. The geyser activity and global rain ceased.

After the rapid horizontal motion stopped, cooling increased the density of the new ocean floor, producing gradually deepening oceans. This took the Flood waters back into the oceans and eventually produced our current ocean basins.

REFERENCES

S. Austin et al., "Catastrophic plate tectonics: a global Flood model of earth history," *Third International Conference on Creationism,* Creation Science Fellowship, Pittsburgh, Pennsylvania, pp. 6–9, 622, 1994.

J. Baumgardner, "Runaway subduction as the driving mechanism for the Genesis Flood," *Proceedings of the Third International Conference on Creationism,* Creation Science Fellowship, Pittsburgh, pp. 63–76, 1994.

A. Snelling, "Plate tectonics: have the continents really moved apart?" *Creation Technical Journal,* **9**(1):12–19, 1995.

The Fossil Record

- 95% of all fossils are marine invertebrates, particularly shellfish.
- Of the remaining 5%, 95% are algae and plant fossils (4.75%).
- Of the remaining 0.25%, 95% consist of the other invertebrates, including insects (0.2375%).
- The remaining 0.0125% includes all vertebrates, mostly fish. 95% of the few land vertebrates consist of less than one bone. (For example, only about 1,200 dinosaur skeletons have been found.) 95% of the mammal fossils were deposited during the Ice Age.
- The fossil record is best understood as the result of a marine cataclysm that utterly annihilated the continents and land dwellers (Genesis 7:18–24; 2 Peter 3:6).

FOSSIL GRAVEYARDS

LINCOLN COUNTY, WYOMING

Alligator, fish of many species, turtles, mammals, mollusks, crustaceans, insects and 6–8 ft palm leaves buried together

SHALES, CALIFORNIA

More than 1 billion herring fossils in a 4-square-mile area

MONTCEAU-LES-MINES, FRANCE

Hundreds of thousands of fossils, marine creatures buried with amphibians, spiders, scorpions, millipedes, insects and reptiles

FLORISSANT, FLORIDA

Wide variety of insects, freshwater mollusks, fish, birds and several hundred plant species buried together

KAROO FORMATION, SOUTH AFRICA

More than 300 species identified: algae, single-celled marine animals, corals, brachiopods, sea urchins, decomposed wood, shark's teeth, skull of a toothed whale and marsupial opossum

COAL LAYERS WORLDWIDE

Probably more than 7 trillion tons of coal from at least that quantity of vegetation

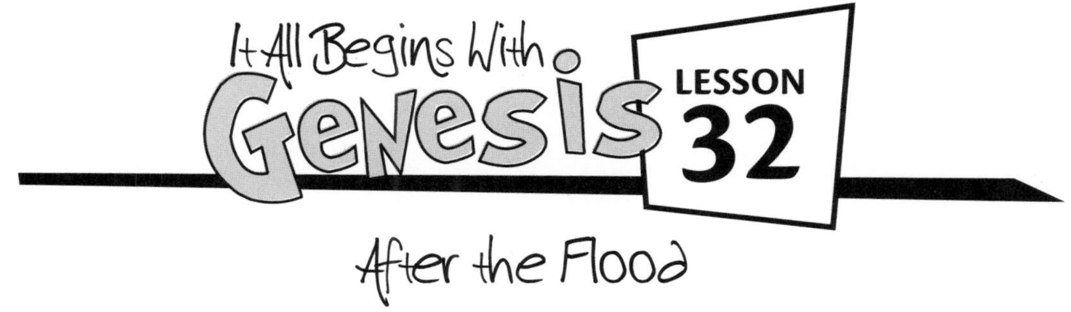

After the Flood

Scripture: Genesis 9; Job passages

Suggested memory verse:

Genesis 9:15

What this lesson is about:

This lesson begins with Genesis 9 and God's covenant with the entire created order. It touches briefly on the subject of capital punishment. It addresses the years following the Flood, and includes theories about post-Flood catastrophism and the Ice Age. Biblical and naturalistic worldviews are contrasted.

7 C's Connection: Catastrophe

Goals for the lesson: The student should

- understand what Genesis 9 has to say about the fear of animals and the permission to eat meat.
- understand what Genesis 9 has to say about the death penalty.
- be able to define the word 'covenant.'
- know the sign and provisions of the Noahic covenant.
- be able to speculate upon the catastrophes found in the earth record that relate to the immediate post-Flood period.

Preparation for lesson:

- Work through the student's lesson 32.
- Observation sheet of Genesis 9
- Illustration showing the new world after the Flood (illustration 32-1 on the curriculum CD)
- Pictures from books of volcanoes, earthquakes, glaciers (or use illustration 32-2 on the curriculum CD)
- Illustration of the Ice Age (illustration 32-3 on the CD)
- Worldview eyeglasses

After the Flood

Plan for lesson:

- **Introduction.** Explain that we are going to try to understand something about what it might have been like to come off the Ark and face a new world. Ask the students to speculate about what Noah and his family must have faced.
- **Class work and discussion.** Instruct the students to take out their worksheet for Genesis 9 and read verses 1–4. God is speaking to Noah. Ask them what command to Noah sounds like something God also said to Adam. *(Be fruitful, multiply, fill the earth.)* Then ask them what God said to Noah that is something new and different. *(fear and terror put into animals, permission to eat meat instead of only plants)* They may wish to share ideas of why that permission might have been necessary at that time in history. *(possible answers: lack of necessary vegetation, change in climate that would require more protein)*
- **Class work and discussion.** Ask the class to read Genesis 9:4–7 and mark the key word 'blood.' Ask them to tell you in their own words what God is instituting in these verses. *(capital punishment)* Ask them if they remember from earlier study in Genesis why blood is so important to God. *(The life of the flesh is in the blood.)* As you discuss capital punishment, be sure they see why it was instituted—have them circle verse 6. Ask if God did this because life wasn't important or because He was placing a very high value on human life.
- **Class work and discussion.** Now direct the class to 9:8–17. Have them mark 'covenant' throughout. Explain that this is a very important concept in Scripture and that God works through covenants. They may be able to tell you of some other covenants: the Abrahamic covenant, the Mosaic covenant and the New Covenant in Christ. As you go through the marking of the word, show what questions about the Noahic covenant are answered. Then ask them to fill in the chart found in their lesson.
- **Teaching about the post-Flood physical world.** Spend a little time allowing the class to speculate about what life would have been like in those early years following the Flood—how they would build homes, find food, etc.

  Tell them also that the world they found was different from the world God created originally or the world we experience today. Ask them what happens after someone hits a big gong—do the effects of the sound continue to linger? Or imagine that a 5,000 lb weight was put on top of you for a year (and you miraculously survived). Once the weight was removed, would you need to make some residual adjustments before you were 'normal' again? The same is true for an event that was so catastrophic, only 4,500 years ago. Many creation scientists believe that all the earthquakes, hurricanes, volcanoes, etc. we experience today are simply residual effects of the Flood.

Three major observations about the post-Flood world:

1. Many catastrophes. (Illustrate with pictures of earthquakes and volcanoes—see illustration 32-2 on the curriculum CD.) We know from the rock record that there are many more earthquakes, volcanoes and meteor impacts reflected in the Flood sediments than anything before or since. For example, Yellowstone National Park is located in one collapsed volcano. We also have evidence of mountains that were cut off at the roots and vibrated many miles from their source (near San Diego and elsewhere).
2. Warm oceans/cold continents. Use the Ice Age illustration (32-3) found in the curriculum CD. Discuss how the Ice Age could have begun. Direct students to the quotes from Job found in their lesson and let them tell you what kind of catastrophe the verses allude to. Ice and snow were things that Job had been familiar with.
3. More water. The excess water from the Flood provided a wetter earth than we know now. For example, we know that in Abraham's time the valley near Sodom and Gomorrah was a lush area because Lot chose to move there with his family and flocks. Today that region is a desert.

(At the end of this guide, for the teacher's information, are two brief articles by Dr. Kurt Wise that address post-Flood catastrophism, repopulation and the Ice Age. They may help clarify some points that will help you teach this material.)

- **Summary.** In closing, bring out your two pairs of eyeglasses and ask how each would view the Ice Age.

  The *naturalistic worldview* would deny there was a worldwide Flood at all. He believes there were a series of Ice Ages that continued for many millions of years. He does not have a scientific explanation for how they could have occurred.

  The *biblical worldview* would recognize only one Ice Age in the first centuries following the Flood. Warm oceans and cold continents can explain the mechanism of the Ice Age.

- **Activity.** In the remaining time, have the students draw pictures of the post-Flood world. They could be added to the ongoing biblical time line.
- Note: A section of the student lesson deals with Genesis 9:20–29 (pp. 188–189). It covers Noah's drunkenness and the curse and prophecy that followed. This section can be held for the following lesson if time is limited. It will relate well to the genealogy of the sons of Noah and can be included with this section. If you have time, however, it would be good to go through this section with your class.

If you have additional time . . .
Suggestions for augmenting lessons (home school, day school)

One or two extra sessions are recommended. More time is needed for orderly observation of chapter 9 and the reinforcement of inductive study principles. Additional sessions integrated with earth science would include the Ice Age, woolly mammoths, volcanoes and earthquakes.

Dr. Kurt Wise's lecture 10 "The post-Flood world'" in *Genesis Part 2* would also increase understanding here. Answers in Genesis has several sources available, such as *The New Answers Book 1* (see chapters 11 and 16), the DVD *Ice Age: Only the Bible Explains It*, and Michael and Beverly Oard's delightfully illustrated books *Life in the Great Ice Age* and *Uncovering the Mysterious Woolly Mammoth* (available from www.AnswersInGenesis.org).

This would also be an appropriate time for a Zonk game review of the Flood chapters.

RESIDUAL CATASTROPHISM:

Are the effects of the Flood present today?

by Dr. Kurt P. Wise

If Noah's Flood occurred anything like the manner which catastrophic plate tectonics suggests (see article at the end of the previous lesson), then the catastrophism of the Flood did not end the day Noah set foot off the Ark. Although the earth's mantle can be pushed aside and circulated rather quickly (at perhaps meters per second), it responds much, much more slowly when being pressed down or pulled up. A marble placed on top of molasses would sink into the molasses because of its greater weight—fast at first and more slowly as it got near its final position. So also, if a very large iron meteorite were laid on the earth's surface, the meteorite would sink into the earth—more quickly at first and then more slowly with time. Because the earth's mantle is so viscous (thick), it takes about 25,000 years for the completion of this kind of sinking. Therefore, even after the rapid motions of the Flood were over, it should take close to 25,000 years for all the vertical adjustments to end. Since that much time has not occurred since the Flood, it can be assumed that *modern geologic activity is merely leftover activity from the Flood*.

It can also be assumed that immediately after the Flood, especially for the first centuries, the geologic activity would have been quite dramatic indeed. It is likely that *large earthquakes* and *volcanic eruptions* occurred on a daily basis after the Flood. It is also likely that the magnitude of these events was most likely much greater than we experience in the present. As an example, Yellowstone National Park was probably erupting during this period of time. Most of the park is within a *single* volcanic cone—*many* times larger than the largest volcanoes we are familiar with today. Another example comes from the valley and ridge province of southern California, southwestern Nevada and western Arizona. There it is possible that most mountains are not in their original location—each broke off from its original root and vibrated across the earth's surface by virtually continuous earthquake activity during the early post-Flood period. It is likely that many of the world's tall mountains (e.g. the Alps, the Himalayas, the Rockies, the Andes and even the mountains of Ararat) and substantial plateaus (e.g. the Colorado and Tibetan Plateaus) *rose* hundreds to thousands of feet, and that some of the earth's most substantial valleys (for example, the Dead Sea and the East African rifts) *dropped* during this amazing period of time. Some of the evidence of recent past vertical motions can be seen in the Andes irrigation systems, which have risen dozens to hundreds of feet from their original position since they were built. Other evidence is shown on the many Andean beaches that have risen thousands of feet above sea level during the post-Flood years.

For more information

S. Austin et al., "Catastrophic plate tectonics: a global model of earth history," *Third International Conference on Creationism*, Creation Science Fellowship, Pittsburgh, pp. 609–622, 1994.

THE ICE ADVANCE

by Dr Kurt P. Wise

Conditions contributing to an Ice Age

According to oxygen-isotope ratios in fossil shells, average ocean temperatures *increased* throughout what are thought to be Flood sediments to between 25 and 30 degrees centigrade—between 20 and 25 degrees centigrade over pre-Flood and current temperatures. The warm ocean water after the Flood generated unusual climatic conditions. The air over the continents, which can cool off more readily at night by radiation into space, was *cool and dry*. Because of the warmth of the oceans, the air over the oceans was *warm and wet*. This is thought to have caused a rather brisk and perhaps continuous motion of warm wet air off the oceans onto the land. The evaporation of the ocean water to replace the air moving onto the continents served to cool the oceans, and the continents served to cool the moisture-laden air, causing abundant rainfall.

The ocean-to-land gradient was possibly so great as to produce two 'hypercanes'—one over the North Atlantic and one over the South Pacific. A hypercane is an extremely large hurricane (perhaps covering an eighth of the earth's surface) that remains at a particular location for long periods of time. In the case of the post-Flood hypercanes, they *may have persisted for five to ten centuries after the Flood*. During their existence they would cause both *cooling of the oceans* and tremendous *precipitation over the continents*.

Results of the climatic change

Areas of the earth's surface that are now dry were well-watered during this period. (Evidence for this includes forests and river valleys buried under the desert sands of the Sahara, water erosion evidence on the Sphinx, a green Dead Sea Valley during the time of Lot and huge ramps of sediment—pediments and huge alluvial fans—off desert mountains such as those in Death Valley.) Large lakes were developed in many areas during this time period (such as the lake of which the Great Salt Lake is only a small evaporated remnant, and the Hopi and Canyonlands Lakes thought to have been the water source for the erosion of the Grand Canyon). The world's great deltas (for example, the Mississippi, Amazon, Nile, Niger, Yangtze and Braumaputra river deltas), which reach far out into the oceans, were eroded during this period of time. Also during this time organisms spread from the Ark to populate the entire world. Given the fact that along all the world's oceans there was a nice climatic gradient from humid tropical (close to the ocean) to dry subarctic (away from the ocean), organisms could migrate in comfortable climates to any location on earth.

Towards the end of this period, the ocean (and earth) temperatures would have dropped sufficiently for the precipitation to fall as snow at high elevations (in the mountains) and in high-latitude regions under the hypercanes (e.g. Greenland, Eastern Canada and Antarctica). The rate of precipitation was too high to allow melting of the snow, and thus it quickly accumulated as ice. Probably between 500 and 1,000 years after the Flood the ice had accumulated sufficient thickness to begin to surge under its own weight, rapidly moving away from the accumulation centers in pulses.

What time frame?

The actual ice advance and subsequent melting may have occurred in only decades of time. The rapid advance explains why such large areas of land once covered by ice (e.g. the States of Illinois, Indiana and Ohio) show very little to no evidence of rebounding from ice loading (because the ice did not stay long enough to weigh those areas down). It also explains the lack of fossil organisms in the sediments between the ice advances. The rapid melting also explains the many evidences of catastrophic flooding from glacial meltwaters (such as, the Bonneville Flood to produce the channeled scablands of eastern Washington and the Columbia River gorge, and the Kankakee Flood, which produced the Illinois River Gorge, etc.). The floating and rapid freezing of large amounts of glacial meltwater over the North Polar Ocean also explains the fresh-water ice cap found over the North Pole. Future research may even provide an explanation for the frozen tundra and frozen bodies of large animals (such as the mammoth) found in the frozen mud of high northern latitudes.

For more information

M. Oard, *An Ice Age Caused by the Genesis Flood*, Institute for Creation Research, El Cajon, California, 1990.

L. Vardiman, "A conceptual transition model of the atmospheric global circulation following the Genesis Flood," in R. Walsh (Ed.), *Proceedings of the Third International Conference on Creationism*, Creation Science Fellowship, Pittsburgh, pp. 569–579, 1994.

THE REPOPULATION OF THE WORLD

by Dr Kurt P. Wise

According to Scripture, the land animals and man had to repopulate the earth from the Ark. The Ark was located in the mountains of Ararat. Interestingly, computer calculations of the place on earth that would require the least total distribution distance (i.e. the geographic center of the continents) is located in the Middle East, not far from the mountains of Ararat. The Ark was therefore guided to the most efficient place from which to repopulate the earth. Also, as indicated in the previous 'Ice Advance' article, the post-Flood earth probably had a warm ocean and cool continents. This would leave a zone of climates along all the oceans (warm near the ocean and cool away from it), which would allow an organism of any climatic preference to move through all the latitudes to virtually any shoreline in the world.

Post-Flood population increases were probably much higher than we have traditionally assumed. Modern rates of human population growth projected into the past would allow for the present population of humans in about 5,000 years. This is not only more time than has elapsed since the Flood, but it is also assuming that humans did not live the longer life spans listed in Genesis 11. This would suggest that post-Flood human populations grew at a *faster* rate than is observed at present. It is likely that there are internally designed mechanisms in the DNA of organisms (including humans) that allow for different rates of reproduction under different circumstances. It is well-known, for example, that the number of male births increased substantially after World War II, as if there were some internal mechanism that responded to the loss of males in the population. Experiments on deer have also shown that a pregnant doe shown too many deer per unit time will tend to abort her fetus, and a doe shown too few deer per unit time will tend to undergo multiple ovulation. After the eruption of Mount Saint Helens, the twin and triplet production in the devastated elk population substantially increased. As a result, the elk population rebounded much more rapidly than had been expected. It may well be that many or most organisms have mechanisms created by God that allow them to respond quickly when populations are much smaller than the land can sustain.

Many people have doubted the Flood scenario because the spreading of so many animals from the Ark to the uttermost parts of the earth seems impossible—certainly, it is reasoned, it would be impossible for some organisms. On that point it is important to note that representatives of each *kind* (or *baramin*) of land animal were taken onto the Ark. This means that among all the different species within a given *baramin,* the one God chose to place on the Ark might well have been the species most capable of long-distance migration. Furthermore, most animal families (likely corresponding to baramins) are distributed globally. This means that the original *baramin* might have spread widely and then speciated at different places in its range. It also must be noted that among the animal families that are *not* distributed globally (e.g. Australian marsupial families), there is often a fossil record that shows a global or near-global distribution in the past, with living populations separated from others by extinction.

As the 'ice advance' approached, ocean water was transferred to glacial ice on the continent. This caused the draining of shallow seas and the exposure of land bridges to now water-locked land areas. Land bridges—connecting Asia and Alaska (across the Bering Sea), connecting many Malaysian and Indonesian islands with Southeast Asia and connecting England with Europe—probably facilitated migration to these areas.

Other modes of transportation that need further investigation are plant mat flotation and human transportation (intentionally and unintentionally). Noah's ancestors had obviously inherited boat-building skills, which they would utilize as they migrated.

If recent research is typical, further research should resolve most if not all the difficulties with a recent global repopulation scenario.

For further information (available from Answers in Genesis, see www.AnswersInGenesis.org)

M. Oard *An Ice Age Caused by the Genesis Flood*, Institute for Creation Research, El Cajon, California, 1990.

It All Begins With Genesis

LESSON 33

Different languages, peoples, nations?

Scripture: Genesis 10–11

Suggested memory verse:

Acts 17:26

What this lesson is about:

This lesson overviews Genesis 10 and 11. The focus is the events surrounding the Tower of Babel on the plain of Shinar.

7 C's Connection: Confusion

Goals for the lesson: The student should

- understand how chapters 10 and 11 relate to one another.
- know the origin of the languages and nations of the earth.
- be able to identify Nimrod and his place in history.

Preparation for lesson:

- Work through the student's lesson 33.
- Observation sheets for Genesis 10 and 11
- Small squares of paper. Half should be marked with a large 'M' and the other half with a small 'm.'
- Read *The New Answers Book 1* (chapter 17) 'Are there Really Different Races?' There is an excerpt found at the end of this teacher lesson and the full article can be read online at www.answers-ingenesis.org/go/races.

Plan for lesson:

- **Introduction and teaching.** Help the class see the context of Genesis 10. Ask the students to take out their observation worksheets for chapters 10 and 11. Spend a few moments helping them to see the content of the chapters (the genealogies of Shem, Ham and Japheth) and to see that the events of Babel in chapter 11 actually precede the events of chapter 10.
- **Class work and discussion**. The first four pages of the student lesson focus on the events of Genesis 11:1–9. Direct the students to that passage. You can either assign the questions as class work and later discuss them, or take the students through the questions and discuss them as

you go. Use an illustration of Genesis 11 as a point of reference. It would be fun for the discussion if you would dramatize in some fashion what it is like to be in a place where everyone speaks a language you don't understand.

Activity. Write on the board the question 'How many races are in the world today?' and give a choice of 1, 3, 5 or 'more than 15.' Most of the students will choose 'more than 15.' Point out that there is only one 'race'—the human race. Tell them there are many 'people groups,' but only one species: *Homo sapiens sapiens.* The differences in genetics are very, very small. Most differences that you find in people groups are due to culture, not genetics.

Illustrate using color of skin as an example. Point out that everyone has the same pigment (melanin) in his or her skin. However, because of genetics, some have more melanin than others and therefore are darker.

Give each student a slip of paper with either a large 'M' or small 'm' on it. Ask them to 'pair up' with someone else in the room. (Depending on the class, you may want to pair up boys with girls or friends with friends.)

Once they are in pairs, tell them to pretend one is a father and one is a mother and they have a child. We're going to talk about what color of skin their child will have.

Ask for those who have two big 'M's to go to one side of the room. They are the pairs who have dark, or 'black,' skins.

Ask for those who have two little 'm's to go to the other side of the room. They have 'white' skins.

Those who have a big 'M' and a little 'm' stay in the middle. They have brown skin.

Point out that if all the groups stay together, the m's will continue to be shifted around, and all skin shades will be in the population (as in India today, where there are sometimes white, black and brown skins in a single family.)

But suppose you move far away from other populations, and all you have are people with a 'big M'? The result will always be black skin, because these people have lost the gene for small 'm.' The same is true for white skins because they have lost the 'big M' genes.

Ask how long it would take to have black, brown and white groups of people. *(one generation)*

This may give you opportunity to talk about racial conflict today, and how very unbiblical it is. The various people groups are all relatives of Noah. Skin color and other seemingly 'distinctive' traits of a particular group represent an infinitely small part of the human DNA. (It is interesting to point out that there are indeed no different shaped eyes. All eyeballs are the same. However, certain people groups have more fat in the eyelid, which results in different appearances.)

- **Class work and discussion.** Assign the questions about Nimrod found on pages 194–195. Discuss their answers.
- Finally, if time remains, instruct the students to circle the theme and draw the pictures at the end of each observation sheet. It would be helpful to attach some of the pictures to your ongoing time-line project, indicating an important time in post-Flood history.

If you have additional time . . .
Suggestions for augmenting lessons (home school, day school)

One extra session would be helpful in order to allow the students to work individually through their chapter 10 and 11 worksheets. Additional sessions related to genetics could be integrated with the life science class.

There are two good 'race' videos in the *Answers ... with Ken Ham* seminar series: 'Where Do the Races Come From?' and 'Genesis: Today's Answer to Racism' (available on DVD from www.AnswersInGenesis.org). *The New Answers Book 1* (chapter 17) provides additional information on races and *The New Answers Book 2* (chapter 28) discusses the events surrounding the dispersion at Babel.

ARE THERE REALLY DIFFERENT RACES?

(Condensed from chapter 17 of *The New Answers Book 1* by Ken Ham, Master Books, 2006. Used by permission.)

What Constitutes a "Race"?

In the 1800s, before Darwinian evolution was popularized, most people, when talking about "races," would be referring to such groups as the "English race," "Irish race," and so on. However, this all changed in 1859 when Charles Darwin published his book *On the Origin of Species by Means of Natural Selection or the Preservation of Favoured Races in the Struggle for Life.*

Darwinian evolution was (and still is) inherently a racist philosophy, teaching that different groups or "races" of people evolved at different times and rates, so some groups are more like their apelike ancestors than others. Leading evolutionist Stephen Jay Gould claimed, "Biological arguments for racism may have been common before 1859, but they increased by orders of magnitude following the acceptance of evolutionary theory."

Racist attitudes fueled by evolutionary thinking were largely responsible for an African pygmy being displayed, along with an orangutan, in a cage in the Bronx zoo. Indeed, Congo pygmies were once thought to be "small apelike, elfish creatures" that "exhibit many ape-like features in their bodies."

As a result of Darwinian evolution, many people started thinking in terms of the different people groups around the world representing different "races," but within the context of evolutionary philosophy. This has resulted in many people today, consciously or unconsciously, having ingrained prejudices against certain other groups of people.

However, all human beings in the world today are classified as *Homo sapiens sapiens*. Scientists today admit that, biologically, there really is only one race of humans. For instance, a scientist at the Advancement of Science Convention in Atlanta stated, "Race is a social construct derived mainly from perceptions conditioned by events of recorded history, and it has no basic biological reality." This person went on to say, "Curiously enough, the idea comes very close to being of American manufacture."

Personally, because of the influences of Darwinian evolution and the resulting prejudices, I believe everyone (and especially Christians) should abandon the term "race(s)." We could refer instead to the different "people groups" around the world.

The Bible and "Race"

The Bible does not even use the word race in reference to people, but it does describe all human beings as being of "one blood" (Acts 17:26). This of course emphasizes that we are all related, as all humans are descendants of the first man, Adam (1 Corinthians 15:45), who was created in the image of God (Genesis 1:26–27). The Last Adam, Jesus Christ (1 Corinthians 15:45) also became a descendant of Adam. Any descendant of Adam can be saved because our mutual relative by blood (Jesus Christ) died and rose again. This is why the gospel can (and should) be preached to all tribes and nations.

"Racial" Differences

But some people think there must be different races of people because there appear to be major differences between various groups, such as skin color and eye shape.

The truth, though, is that these so-called "racial characteristics" are only minor variations among people groups. If one were to take any two people anywhere in the world, scientists have found that the basic genetic differences between these two people would typically be around 0.2 percent—even if they came from the same people group. But these so-called "racial" characteristics that people think are major differences (skin color, eye shape, etc.) "account for only 0.012 percent of human biological variation."

In other words, the so-called "racial" differences are absolutely trivial— overall, there is more variation within any group than there is between one group and another. The only reason many people think these differences are major is because they've been brought up in a culture that has taught them to see the differences this way.

If the Bible teaches and science confirms that all are of the same human race and all are related as descendants of Adam, then why are there such seemingly great differences between us (for example, in skin color)? The answer, again, comes with a biblically informed understanding of science.

Skin "Color"

Jesus loves the little children, all the children of the world. Red and yellow, black and white, they are precious in His sight.

When Jesus said, "Let the little children come to Me, and do not forbid them; for of such is the kingdom of heaven" (Matthew 19:14), He did not distinguish between skin colors. In fact, scientists have discovered that there is one major pigment, called melanin, that produces our skin color. There are two main forms of melanin: eumelanin (brown to black) and pheomelanin (red to yellow). These combine to give us the particular shade of skin that we have.

Melanin is produced by melanocytes, which are cells in the bottom layer of the epidermis. No matter what our shade of skin, we all have approximately the same concentration of melanocytes in our bodies. Melanocytes insert melanin into melanosomes, which transfer the melanin into other skin cells, which are capable of dividing (stem cells), primarily in the lowest layer of the epidermis.

The melanosomes (tiny melanin-packaging units) are slightly larger and more numerous per cell in dark-skinned than light skinned people. They also do not degrade as readily, and disperse into adjacent skin cells to a higher degree.

In the stem cells, the pigment serves its function as it forms a little dark umbrella over each nucleus. The melanin protects the epidermal cells from being damaged by sunlight. In people with lighter shades of skin, much of the pigment is lost after these cells divide and their daughter cells move up in the epidermis to form the surface dead layer—the stratum corneum.

Geneticists have found that four to six genes, each with multiple alleles (or variations), control the amount and type of melanin produced. Because of this, a wide variety of skin shades exist. In fact, it is quite easy for one couple to produce a wide range of skin shades in just one generation, as will be shown below.

Inheritance

DNA (deoxyribonucleic acid) is the molecule of heredity that is passed from parents to child. In humans, the child inherits 23 chromosomes from each parent (the father donates 23 through his sperm, while the mother donates 23 through her egg). At the moment of conception, these chromosomes unite to form a unique combination of DNA and control much of what makes the child an individual. Each chromosome pair contains hundreds of genes, which regulate the physical development of the child. Note that no new genetic information is generated at conception, but a new combination of already-existing genetic information is formed.

To illustrate the basic genetic principles involved in determining skin shade, we'll use a simplified explanation, with just two genes controlling the production of melanin. Let's say that the A and B versions of the genes code for a lot of melanin, while the a and b versions code for a small amount of melanin.

If the father's sperm carried the AB version and the mother's ovum carried the AB, the child would be AABB, with a lot of melanin, and thus very dark skin. Should both parents carry the ab version, the child would be aabb, with very little melanin, and thus very light skin. If the father carries AB (very dark skin) and the mother carries ab (very light skin), the child will be AaBb, with a middle brown shade of skin. In fact, the majority of the world's population has a middle brown skin shade.

A simple exercise with a Punnet Square shows that if each parent has a middle brown shade of skin (AaBb), the combinations that they could produce result in a wide variety of skin shades in just one generation. Based on the skin colors seen today, we can infer that Adam and Eve most likely would have had a middle brown skin color. Their children, and children's children, could have ranged from very light to very dark.

No one really has red, or yellow, or black skin. We all have the same basic color, just different shades of it. We all share the same pigments—our bodies just have different combinations of them.

Origin of People Groups

We know that Adam and Eve were the first two people. Their descendants filled the earth. However, the world's population was reduced to eight during the Flood of Noah. From these eight individuals have come all the tribes and nations. It is likely that the skin shade of Noah and his family was middle brown. This would enable his sons and their wives to produce a variety of skin shades in just one generation. Because there was a common language and everybody lived in the same general vicinity, barriers that may have prevented their descendants from freely intermarrying weren't as great as they are today. Thus, distinct differences in features and skin color in the population weren't as prevalent as they are today.

In Genesis 11 we read of the rebellion at the Tower of Babel. God judged this rebellion by giving each family group a different language. This made it impossible for the groups to understand each other, and so they split apart, each extended family going its own way, and finding a different place to live. The result was that the people were scattered over the earth.

Because of the new language and geographic barriers, the groups no longer freely mixed with other groups, and the result was a splitting of the gene pool. Different cultures formed, with certain features becoming predominant within each group.

Some of these (skin color, eye shape, and so on) became general characteristics of each particular people group through various selection pressures (environmental, sexual, etc.) and/or mutation. For example, because of the protective factor of melanin, those with darker skin would have been more likely to survive in areas where sunlight is more intense (warmer, tropical areas near the equator), as they are less likely to suffer from diseases such as skin cancer.

The Dispersion at Babel

Note that the context of Genesis 11 makes it clear that the reason for God's scattering the people over the earth was that they had united in rebellion against Him. We need to understand that the sovereign creator God is in charge of the nations of this world. Paul makes this very clear in Acts 17:26. As John Gill makes clear in his classic commentary, the context is that God is in charge of all things—where, how, and for how long any person, tribe, or nation will live, prosper, and perish.

In all of this, God is working to redeem for Himself a people who are one in Christ. The Bible makes clear in Galatians 3:28, Colossians 3:11, and Romans 10:12–13 that in regard to salvation, there is no distinction between male or female or Jew or Greek. In Christ, any separation between people is broken down. As Christians, we are one in Christ and thus have a common purpose—to live for Him who made us.

Conclusion

The church could greatly relieve the tensions over racism (particularly in countries like America), if only the leaders would teach biblical truths about our shared ancestry: all people are descended from one man and woman; all people are equal before God; all are sinners in need of salvation; all need to build their thinking on God's Word and judge all their cultural aspects accordingly; all need to be one in Christ and put an end to their rebellion against their Creator.

It All Begins With Genesis

LESSON 34

God's plan for His world unfolds

Scripture: Genesis 9–11

Suggested memory verse: (same verse as lesson 33)

Acts 17:26

What this lesson is about:

This lesson traces the sons of Noah throughout the nations of the world. It shows God's plan for Christ to come through Shem and through the line of Abraham.

7 C's Connection: Confusion

Goals for the lesson: The student should

- see how the various nations formed by the sons of Noah.
- follow Christ's genealogy from Shem through Abraham.
- be able to summarize what it means to have a biblical view of the world.

Preparation for lesson:

- Work through the student's lesson 34.
- To prepare three genealogy posters, you need

  Poster board
  3x5 index cards with names of each person/nation in the genealogies. Color sons of Japheth blue, sons of Ham green and sons of Shem yellow.
  Glue or tape
  Black marker to draw lines on the posters
  Map (Enlarge the black-and-white map in the student lesson, or use the color map on the curriculum CD, labeled 34-1.)
  Pens or highlighters—blue, green and yellow

Plan for lesson:

- **Review** with the students what they learned last week about how the people on the earth were divided.
- **Class work.** If your class size is very small, you can follow the instructions in the lesson and have the students complete their pages as directed. However, if you have a large enough class, the following group project would be an enjoyable way to study the genealogies.

- Divide the class into three groups. Group 1 represents Japheth, group 2 represents Ham, and group 3 represents Shem.
- Give each group a piece of poster board that you have labeled Shem, Ham or Japheth. Give each group your prepared index cards with the names of the genealogy. Include glue or tape for attaching the names. Instruct the group to look at the appropriate section of Genesis 10 (Shem's group will have to look at Genesis 11 as well) and put the family tree together.
- When each group has completed their poster, instruct them to mark the places on the map that are part of their particular genealogy. They should mark their own personal maps and also mark the large map for the time-line bulletin board.
- When they finish coloring their part of the map, they should look to the big map on the board and color in the places that the other groups completed.
- **Discussion.** Post the three genealogy posters in front of the class and discuss each. Begin by going to Genesis 9 and discussing the prophecy of Noah concerning the three sons.

  Other discussion topics could include:

  What son of Noah were you descended from?
  What can you remember about Nimrod?
  Who were the Canaanites?
  Why is the genealogy of Shem so important?
  Did you notice what happened to the ages of the people listed in Shem's line?

- **Conclusions.** Since this is the last lesson of the course, it would be helpful to spend some time pulling together the threads of the course—why Genesis is foundational, and the worldview it has provided. You might go through the major worldview questions covered by the course and ask students how Genesis gives them what they need to give sound answers.

  Who is God?
  Who is man? What makes me special?
  What is the purpose for my life?
  How can we explain sin, sorrow, suffering?
  What does the future hold?

  You might prefer to save one whole day at the end of the course to have a final Zonk review. Some suggested Zonk questions are included at the end of this lesson for your use, if desired.

If you have additional time . . .
Suggestions for augmenting lessons (home school, day school)

One or two extra sessions should be added for final review of concepts and the Zonk game.

Final Zonk questions

100-point questions

What are the six questions asked of the biblical text in inductive Bible study?
When you began the year and took a helicopter ride over the first 11 chapters of Genesis, getting the 'big picture,' what step of inductive study were you doing? (*overview*)
The *main* reason we studied science this year was (a) to refute evolution; (b) to know more about natural selection, mutations, geology, etc.; (c) to know the Creator better by studying His creation.
When someone believes in intelligent design, what worldview is this? (*theistic)*
When someone believes in natural selection, what worldview is this? *(both theistic and naturalistic)*
When someone believes in evolution, what worldview is this? Can a person be a Christian if he believes in evolution? (*naturalistic; yes he can still be a Christian if he believes Jesus came and died for his sins)*
When someone believes that the rock layers and fossils of the earth were laid down by a huge catastrophe in the days of Noah, what worldview is this? (*biblical)*
When someone believes the rock layers and fossils of the earth were laid down by uniformitarian processes over billions of year, what worldview is this? *(naturalistic)*
When someone believes that species can form, what worldview is this? *(both naturalistic and biblical)*
When someone teaches about irreducible complexity in life, what worldview is behind the teaching? *(theistic)*
When someone teaches that all languages and peoples came from the three sons of Noah, what worldview is this? (*biblical*)
How many races are there in the world today? (a) 1 (b) 3 (c) 5 (d) over 10 *(only one—the human race)*
Who was the 'mighty hunter,' a relative of Ham, who established a kingdom in Babel and in Nineveh? (*Nimrod)*
How long did the Flood of Noah last? (a) 40 days and 40 nights (b) 6 months (c) more than 1 year (d) 2 years *(more than 1 year)*

200-point questions

What is inductive Bible study? *(basic answer: the Bible is the first place you go)*
What is a good definition of worldview? *(a total way of looking at your world)*
There are different worldviews around us today. We focused mostly on two different worldviews. What were they? *(naturalistic and biblical or theistic)*
On what Day of Creation were dinosaurs created? *(6)*
On what Day of Creation was man created? *(6)*
On what Day of Creation were the sun, moon and stars created? *(4)*
On what Day of Creation was light created? *(1)*
On what Day of Creation were plants and fruit trees created? *(3)*
On what Day of Creation were the fish and birds created? *(5)*
When did death, disease and struggle for survival come into the world? *(after the Fall in Genesis 3)*
When the headwaiter of the marriage feast of Cana drank the wine that Jesus had created, what kind of a worldview was he demonstrating? (*naturalistic*)
What is the worldview of those who talk about grunting cave men and primitive early civilizations? (*naturalistic*)
Which son of Noah was the ancestor of most of the people in this classroom? *(Japheth)*
From which son of Noah did Christ come? (*Shem*)
From what son of Noah did the Canaanites come? (*Ham*)
From what son of Noah did the Muslims come? (*Shem*)
After Adam and Eve sinned in the Garden, what were the first two emotions they experienced? (*shame and fear*)
When did the first blood sacrifice take place? (*when God made clothes for Adam and Eve in Genesis 3*)
Why did God not accept Cain's offering? (at least two reasons) *(It wasn't a blood sacrifice, it wasn't the first fruits, and he did not have the right heart attitude.)*
What was so wrong about building a tower at Babel? *(emphasis on* ***us,*** *refusal to spread over the earth, setting themselves up as God, not obeying, being rebellious)*
Why did God send the Flood to destroy man? (two reasons) (*violence, thoughts of the heart evil continually, corruption*)
What is the most repeated phrase in Genesis 5? *('and he died')*

300-point questions

When you study the Bible inductively, you do three things. What are they? *(Observe: ask what does it say? Interpret: ask what does it mean? Apply: ask how should I live?)*
What are the four major events that took place in Genesis 1–11?
What do we mean by 'putting the verse in context' in Bible study? *(understanding what comes before and after, how it all fits together, the environment in which the word or passage dwells, and what goes with the text)*
What was the diet prescribed for man and for all animals when they were created? (*vegetables and fruit*) **When did it all change?** (*permission to eat meat after the Flood*)
Name three different kinds of questions whose answers make up your worldview. (*Who is God? Who am I? What is my purpose? What is God like? Where did evil come from?*)
What is the anthropic principle? What worldview would this represent? (*The universe was created with man in mind; theistic.*)
What is baraminology, and what worldview is concerned about it? (*the study of created kinds; theistic*)
Why is blood so important in Scripture? *(the life of the flesh is in the blood)*
Two righteous men were talked about in Genesis 5 (right before the Flood). Who were they? *(Noah and Enoch)*
Are dinosaurs mentioned in the Bible? Where? *(The word wasn't invented yet; they are similar to descriptions found in Job 40; also they were among the land animals that went on the Ark.)*
According to Genesis 7:11, two major things happened at the beginning of the Flood. What were they? (*Fountains of the great deep burst open; the floodgates of the sky were opened, resulting in rain.*)
According to creation scientists today, what is a possible explanation of the source of the Flood waters? *(runaway subduction of the ocean crust; the new ocean crust from the mantle was less dense, forcing ocean waters over land—called catastrophic plate tectonics)*
How would someone with a biblical worldview explain the presence of pain, suffering and catastrophe in the world today?

400-point questions	**Why does your teacher think studying Genesis 1-11 is so important?** (*foundation for the biblical worldview—all Scripture is built on the truths of Genesis*) **What is a presupposition? Give one example.** (*It is something you already believe that influences you in your interpretation of other things. If you believe that the geological layers of rock show evolution, you will interpret every fossil in an evolutionary progression.*) **What does Genesis have to say about capital punishment? When? Why?** (*established in Genesis 9 after the Flood because man is made in the image of God*) **What is the protoevangelium? Where is it found in Genesis?** (*the first announcement of the coming Good News, Genesis 3:15*) **Was Noah a sinner? Why was he considered righteous before God? Give at least two reasons.** (*Though everyone is a sinner, he believed in God, he obeyed God, and he walked with God.*) **Can you give a biblical explanation of how the Grand Canyon might have been formed?** (*receding floodwaters cutting through relatively soft layers of sediments*) **How would you explain cavemen and the use of stone tools in the light of the Bible's teaching about early man?**
500-point questions	**At the beginning of the year and several times after that, you were told that there were three main goals your teacher wanted you to achieve this year. Can you name them?** (*Learn how to study inductively; understand worldviews and build a biblical worldview; understand Genesis 1-11 because it is the foundation of the biblical worldview.*) **When something you are taught in school seems to be in conflict with what you know the Bible teaches, what should you do? (at least 3 things)** (*Go back to Scripture and see for sure what the Bible teaches; recognize the presuppositions and worldview of the one presenting the information; then look for other interpretations that are consistent with Scripture.*) **Define 'uniformitarianism' and 'catastrophism.' What's the difference? What worldview does each represent?**

About the Author

Sheila Richardson has been teaching inductive Bible study for over 30 years, and she spent 12 years 'teaching teachers' as a workshop trainer for Kay Arthur's popular Precept Ministries International (Chattanooga, Tennessee, USA).

In 1996 Sheila co-authored the *Genesis* Bible-study course for Precept Ministries, written with the help of creation scientist, Dr. Kurt Wise.

Burdened about the need for quality materials for young people, Sheila then wrote *It All Begins with Genesis*. She piloted the program to sixth-graders at her church for three years, and then used it as a very successful intergenerational program for another three years. During that period she also authored (with Kurt Wise) "Something from Nothing," designed for high school and early college students. Sheila is the mother of four and grandmother of four. She lives with her family on a farm near Charlottesville, Virginia.